MW00906971

The Elevation of an Industry

50 Years of Select Sires Helping the Cattle Industry Reach New Heights

The Elevation of an Industry

50 Years of Select Sires Helping the Cattle Industry Reach New Heights

by Kirk Sattazahn

© 2015 Kirk Sattazahn

All rights reserved. This book or any portion thereof may not be reproduced or used in any manner whatsoever without the express written permission of the publisher except for the use of brief quotations in a book review.

Layout, Design and Printing by
Post Printing Company
205 W. Fourth St.
Minster, OH 45865

Published by Greyden Press, LLC
2251 Arbor Blvd.
Dayton, OH 45439

First Printing, 2015

ISBN: 978-1-57074-198-2

The Elevation of an Industry
50 Years of Select Sires Helping the Cattle Industry Reach New Heights

High Impact Sires featured

7HO1897	BLACKSTAR		7JE159	SOONER
7HO2236	ELTON		7JE177	DUNCAN
7HO3707	MATHIE		7JE254	BERRETTA
7HO3948	EMORY		7JE535	JACE
7HO4213	INTEGRITY		7JE590	ACTION
7HO5157	DURHAM		164JE1	LEMVIG
7HO5375	BW MARSHALL			
7HO5708	BLITZ		7AY84	BURDETTE
7HO6025	TEAMSTER			
7HO6417	O MAN		7BS750	DYNASTY
7HO6758	MR SAM		7BS752	PRESTIGE
7HO6782	ZENITH		7BS766	AGENDA
7HO7004	DAMION			
7HO7466	MOSCOW		7GU302	GOLIATH
7HO7536	COLDSPRINGS		7GU360	TILLER
7HO7615	COLBY		7GU395	AARON
7HO7838	GLEN			
7HO7872	ADVENT-RED			
7HO8081	PLANET			
7HO8165	MILLION			
7HO8175	PRONTO			
7HO8190	SANCHEZ			
7HO8221	ALEXANDER			
7HO8477	GABOR			
7HO8559	BOGART			
7HO8747	BRONCO			
7HO8856	NIAGRA			
7HO9222	SHOT			
7HO10506	GW ATWOOD			

Dedication

This book is written to celebrate and honor the accomplishments of all the Select Sires federation employees and member-owners who collectively built this industry-leading cooperative. The intent of the author and people interviewed for the book was to honor the entire Select Sires family for the accomplishments of this company through the stories and memories this book creates. While many people are mentioned in this book, space did not allow complete mention of the tremendous number of people who made strong, meaningful and equally important contributions to growth and development of this company. This list of contributors include technicians, sales personnel, technical specialists, production personnel, management, marketing, communications, veterinarians, clerical, shipping, support, maintenance, human resources, finance, IT, international, board members, delegates and many more. Without those people and their contributions, the success of this organization would not have been possible. Our hope is that this book brings back those great memories of friendships, experiences and contributions that make all Select Sires family members proud. The reality of Select Sires success is the result of honorable, dedicated, talented and passionate employees and customer-owners that are the fabric that built this great organization. This book was written to remember those contributions!

Foreword by Horace Backus

Congratulations to Select Sires on its Golden Anniversary, 50 years of service to the cattle breeding industry all across America and throughout the world.

"There is music in history," says an old adage, and that music consists of many songs. The songs could also be called "chapters."

This book contains the "chapters" or "songs" of a great enterprise that has made important music through an immeasurable contribution to the accomplishments of cattle breeders everywhere.

It would seem to be almost a miracle, or even a bit of fiction, that a cooperative of cattle breeders could be blended from many co-ops thus forming a "giant" to serve the industry. Each of the co-ops that joined this group over the years, realized that by so doing, the work of each of them would be made stronger through the whole, and each willingly gave up individual independence to share in that strength.

One basis for measuring the success of Select Sires can be by the amazing number of outstanding sires that have been in the stud. The strength of the stud can also be measured by its equally outstanding staff.

It has been the good fortune of this writer to know the two general managers of the organization for over the latest forty of its fifty-year lifetime, Dick Chichester and Dave Thorbahn.

One can only have a deep respect for their abilities, especially in the choosing of the team that makes up Select. It is impressive that the sire analysts, field staff and people behind the scenes at headquarters have been able to be strong supporters of the industry, with the special ability to get along extremely well with the users of the stud services.

The quality of the bulls that have made their homes at Columbus, Ohio over the years is impressive even beyond the highest hopes and fondest dreams of those who have availed themselves of their use.

When you invoke the names of such Holstein sires as 7HO58 ELEVATION, 7HO980 MARK, 7HO5157 DURHAM, 7HO7872 ADVENT-RED and 7HO10506 GW ATWOOD – you are speaking of breed immortals. While this writer is not familiar with the names of top sires in other breeds, word has always been that that list also contains its full share of breed immortals.

It has not, however, been just the famous star sires that have made the work of Select so valuable to breeders. It is also the depth of the sire lineups, carefully chosen and closely monitored by staff to make sure that each bull is of the right genetics to help all those who use his services and that both the genetic quality and the quality of the physical product meet the highest possible standards.

The chapters to follow constitute an interesting and complete history of Select's great contributions to the cattle breeding world and pay a magnificent tribute to the people and the bulls that have made Select what it is today, and has been for half a century, a leader in its field.

◆ ◆ ◆

A United, Humble Beginning

◆ ◆ ◆

Just east of the Shenadoah River in northern Virginia, where the hills fold together in a never-ending cascade of trees and rolling fields lies a farm in a sleepy hamlet where the most influential sire in the history of bovine breeding was born. It was August 30, 1965 and 7HO58 Round Oak Rag Apple ELEVATION (EX-96-GM) entered the world without a hint of what his impact would be on the Holstein breed, on dairy families around the world and on a group of Artificial Insemination (A.I.) cooperatives that understood that working together would form a bond much stronger than working alone.

Less than 400 miles to the west of Ronald A. Hope's Round Oak Farm where ELEVATION was born, stood a much larger city that would have been a stark contrast to the now rustic birthplace of the up-and-coming bull. Columbus, Ohio was an established American state capital where titans of industry would swing deals every day. A group of three gentlemen representing four mid-American A.I. cooperatives that wanted to incorporate in the state to form a new cooperative would have been considered so uneventful that it didn't even make the business pages for that day. Yet October 12, 1965 did see the birth of Select Sires Inc. when Richard Kellogg, Robert McCormick and P.L. "Lee" Thornbury put pen to paper on the Charter of Incorporation. This started Select Sires on a road hopeful for success with no knowledge of the positive impact on the profitability of customers that the company would eventually come to realize.

The AI industry relied on fresh semen in the early days and deliveries were often made by bus and sometimes by train. Since many AI leaders had been fliers in WWII, all delivery methods were tested, even the occasional air drop.

The fact that Select Sires and ELEVATION were both born in 1965 should be noted as more than just a coincidence. While New Jersey Extension Agent, Enos Perry, is credited for introducing artificial insemination to the masses in 1938, the relatively new process of artificial insemination was just starting to find its role in the success of America's dairy and beef cattle operations. America had finally put World War II and the Korean War in the past and could focus on feeding a hungry world. Dairy farmers around the country were thirsting for more information and more products that could help them maximize output using the limited inputs of their farms. Breed organizations were doing an effective job of showing the possibilities of genetic improvement through planned matings and genetic selection. Now all that was needed was a farmer-led cooperative that focused on getting product from the best sires to the farm for use. Select Sires filled that need.

This is a need that still exists and is still being filled today. Ron Long, Select Mating Service (SMS) evaluator No. 1 (more on that later) clearly states that, "Select Sires is not a bull organization, it is a people organization," a thought that has been echoed many times over the years. It is the people at Select Sires and the farmer-owners that are customers of the cooperative, which have guaranteed that Select Sires has always been responsive to the true needs of the dairy and beef cattle manager. "When our sire committee tells us that calving ease or milk production or some other trait carries more weight in our producer surveys, that is important market research and we look for sires that will meet those needs," shares Charlie Will, current manager of the Holstein sire program.

The cooperative structure that was agreed to in 1965 ensured that feedback and leadership started with the people closest to the product and that has proved to be a seren-dipitous contributor to the success of Select Sires. It is not just the fact that Select Sires is a cooperative that contributes to the direction of the company, but also that Select Sires has a business model that ensures cooperative input from around the country. Whereas a private company might be more focused on profits than on meeting the needs of a customer and a top-heavy cooperative might cater to the needs of hired management or individual board members, the Select Sires federation of cooperative leadership delivers viewpoints from every corner of the country, every type of management style and every type of environment. This belief is also reflected in the Program for Genetic Advance-ment (PGA) young sire sampling program.

Young sire sampling has been the hallmark of the Select Sires philosophy of "a sire for every desire." Just as every new sire that enters the Select Sires program is selected with expectations of being the next great one, the decision to form Select Sires was done with the hope of creating the great ones. The major difference between that new young sire and the formation of Select Sires was the ability of good people to help mold and shape the federation that Select Sires has become. At the time of birth, that new young sire is pretty much locked in with his genetic profile and ability to transmit genes. Sure the analysis of genes will alter slightly as reliability is enhanced with new information, but the ability of the calf to make a difference is already determined. A dynamic, growing company has no such restrictions.

Select Sires was not without growing pains. Just like many fledgling, new organiza-tions have experienced, Select Sires also had its share of missteps. It even had a serious challenge with cash flow that threatened the ability of the company to accomplish its initial goal of helping the American dairy and beef farmer utilize top genetics. But peo-ple can make a difference and Select Sires has always had a knack for finding the right ones. A company for the people and by the people located in a country with the same motto ensured that the best interests of the member-owner were always in focus. First, on acquiring the best sires for members to use, then in developing programs that help the member best utilize the sire through mating and analysis, and finally making sure that the member could stay focused on the traits that really had an ability to return ad-ditional profits by taking care of the basics.

It is probably no coincidence that it was cooperatives from the Midwestern United States that led the way for Select Sires formation. Even today the Midwest has a solid reputation of having down-to-earth people who will wave at you when you are driving by and will quickly chip in to help in a time of need. When the semen exchange pro-gram of Central Ohio Breeders Association (COBA), Kentucky Artificial Breeding As-sociation (KABA) and the Northern and Southern Illinois Breeding Associations grew to a natural result that formed Select Sires, it was just another example of Midwestern cooperation.

Officials of the founding cooperatives felt that a single, jointly owned organization could provide a stronger sire program while also allowing efficiency to be gained in combined production facilities and marketing efforts. There was also a strong feeling that the founding cooperatives should continue with their individual cooperatives so that the local connection was not lost and membership loyalty would remain. Local input is a hallmark of Select Sires to this day.

In October 1965, the founding documents represented a strong desire to gain efficiencies and strength while still keeping a strong connection to the individual member-owner. Degree of ownership in the new cooperative of Select Sires was determined by the contribution of sales from each of the founding members and eight board members (two members from each of the four founding members) formed the first decision-making group. Ownership of sires was transferred to Select Sires but the bulls remained at their original cooperative with Select Sires organizing and contracting appropriate care for each of the animals. The Northern and Southern Illinois Breeding Associations eventually became the Illinois Breeding Co-op and Select Sires' bulls were initially housed in Columbus, Ohio; Hampshire, Ill.; and Breese, Ill. By 1968, no sires were housed at KABA headquarters.

Each member cooperative is responsible for the semen sales in their respective service area. That fact was true in 1965 and still true in 2015. The advantage that the member cooperative has gained is a larger selection of stronger sires to offer their member-owners while purchasing the semen they need directly from Select Sires. The efficiencies at Select Sires help to produce semen in a more economical way than each member cooperative could have done individually and marketing and technical service pieces are standardized for additional efficiencies.

For the first year of operation, Select Sires had no employees. A committee system of employees on loan from the member cooperatives led the new company and worked closely with the farmer-led board of directors in guiding the company to meet the needs of the individual cooperatives that it served. In early 1967, the first permanent management personnel were appointed to be Select Sires employees with many COBA employees making the switch to Select Sires in similar roles. James Mellinger was appointed the first general manager of Select Sires after serving as sales and service manager for COBA.

Over the first two years, the Select Sires sire program owned 125 bulls of all breeds, dairy and beef. There were 67 registered Holstein sires and the cooperative was selling about 850,000 units of semen per year. Holstein sires made up 63 percent of unit sales while 6.5 percent were Jersey, 4.5 percent were Guernsey, 3 percent were Brown Swiss and 1 percent in the Ayrshire breed. Rounding out the sales were beef breeds with 9 percent of the unit sales being Angus, 7 percent being Hereford and Charolais rounding out beef breeds at 3 percent of sales. The Brown Swiss and Ayrshire sires were jointly managed with Eastern A.I. Co-operative in Ithaca, N.Y. The road to growth had begun.

The super highways of today were once cow paths of their own and just as every road needs repaved or has a bump that needs smoothed out, the road Select Sires was on was no different. 1969 proved to be a key year for the federation as six new members joined and the sire program was greatly expanded. The cooperatives that

Retiring General Manager Dick Chichester, (center), is joined by previous General Manager Dr. Jim Nichols and new General Manager Dave Thorbahn at an event given in his honor.

joined the federation included Cache Valley, East Tennessee Artificial Breeding Association, Michigan Area Breeders Cooperative, Mississippi Animal Breeders, Tennessee Artificial Breeding Association and Virginia Artificial Breeding Association. An action list was completed at the July 1969 board meeting with an expectation that a reorganization including the new member cooperatives would be up and functional by September 1, 1969. This reorganization addressed a wide array of decisions from purchasing new sires to identifying service areas and from bringing in additional management personnel to organizing collection schedules for the new combined sire lineup. It was a large undertaking and General Manager Mellinger is to be commended as the additional management team that he hired included three legends that have facilities at Select Sires named for them today: John Hecker, Howard Kellgren and Clif Marshall. Along with this group came the architect for the beef program, Roy Wallace. One final prudent decision made in 1969 was to implement a national young sire sampling program that would be the precursor for the Program for Genetic Advancement (PGA).

The 1970s were an era of growth within the infrastructure of Select Sires but the decade began with some serious challenges. The rapid changes associated with the additional cooperatives joining in 1969 combined with typical growing pains caused real cash flow issues for Select Sires. It was a stressful time and Jim Nichols, Ph.D., was one of the people who came to the right place at the right time when he was named general manager in 1971. An educator by training, he earned a Ph.D. from the University of Minnesota and had a stint as a professor at Penn State University where he coached the dairy judging team to their first national title in 1964. Nichols then moved on to Virginia Tech to serve as head of the dairy science department and eventually became associ-

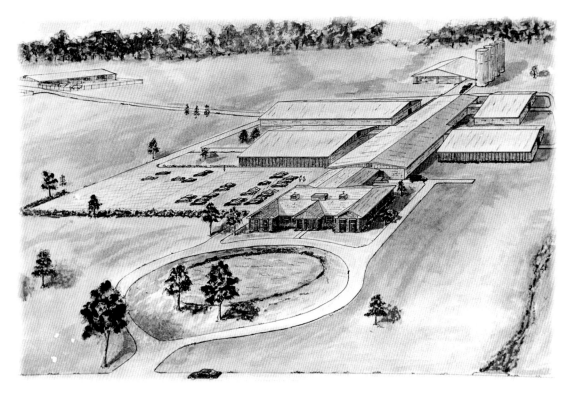

This is an artists rendering of what the new Select Sires facility in Plain City, Ohio would look like. It has since been joined by many additional building projects.

ate dean of the college of agriculture. He garnered respect and his reputation lent great credence to the financially challenged group of cooperatives getting started as Select Sires. Nichols only served as general manager for two years but in that time he initiated two key actions that would chart the course of success for the cooperative. He helped to secure financing from the Louisville Bank for Cooperatives and he started the search for a centralized facility for Select Sires. The financing was a needed lifeline that kept the young company afloat and the building project gave the young company an identity and helped Select Sires become an entity that needed to be taken seriously.

These events might never have occurred had it not been for the controller and secretary-treasurer of Select Sires at the time, Don McKean. Nichols recruited McKean from COBA where he had served as assistant general manager. McKean's financial expertise was crucial in establishing the financial capabilities of Select Sires. His relationship with the Louisville Bank of Cooperatives along with his process for allowing member cooperatives with excess funds to invest in Select Sires provides the time and assets to grow the new federation. In later years, McKean supervised the growth of computer capabilities, provided services to member-cooperatives needing administrative help and developed the pension plan for Select Sires and several member cooperatives, but securing the financing of the building projects was his greatest work.

With a solid base of member cooperatives and people to guide the organization, it was time for Select Sires to plant roots of its own. On June 2, 1972, the company purchased property near Plain City, Ohio to establish a base for the production of semen for the quickly growing national sales force. Along with administration offices to coordinate the marketing of the product, this allowed Select Sires ample land and building space for the housing of bulls as well as the production, processing, packaging, storage and shipping of semen. Up to that point the main office and production facility was the COBA facility near Columbus, Ohio. The new facility allowed Select Sires to establish its own identity as a rapidly growing cooperative focused on the diverse needs of a diverse membership. The new facility was ready for use on January 26, 1973 and was dedicated at a public open house on August 1, 1973. In a bit of irony, General Manager Nichols resigned during that time period on March 30, 1973 due to differences over consolidation within the cooperative. General Manager Dick Chichester began his 27 years of leadership in 1973 and his tremendous influence on the cooperative is covered in his own interview later in the book, but it was evident that Select Sires had turned the corner.

This period of continuous growth and expansion in the Plain City area for Select Sires was remarkable for a cooperative that had been on life support just a few years earlier. As programs would grow and additional facilities were required, the board carefully considered and identified additional opportunities for growth and construction. Fittingly, one of the first major projects was the construction of a sire-in-waiting facility, which was ready for use on September 15, 1974. That building was located at headquarters but it was evident that a separate facility for young sires would be more efficient. On April 5, 1977 Select Sires purchased the Darby Creek farm that became the main sire-in-waiting facility for Select Sires. Eight barns were built and Darby Creek has become synonymous with sire-in-waiting at Select Sires. Now double its original size, the facility was renamed the Hoyt PGA Facility in 2002 in honor of Rodger Hoyt and his contribution to young sire sampling and the PGA at Select Sires.

Building projects continued to satisfy the increasing demand coming in from Select Sires' members domestically and Select Sires partners around the globe. In early 1980, a venture was explored to meet a growing demand for additional genetic products; Select Embryos. On May 13, 1980, Select Embryos Inc., a wholly owned subsidiary of Select Sires was established to produce embryo transfers and to provide additional research on maximizing fertility in dairy cattle. On July 23, 1980, the Freeway Farm was purchased by Select Embryos Inc., to provide new housing for the recipient herd. High profile cattle were brought to Plain City and Select Embryos began intensively producing embryos for dairy farmers across the United States.

Select Embryos had some successful years and provided useful research to the industry about achieving greater success with embryo transfer. However, the embryo market was fickle and success proved fleeting. In 1997, after several negative cash flow years,

The early dairy sire team at Select Sires included Rodger Hoyt, John Hecker, Charlie Will, and Ron Long. The contributions that this team introduced in the form of bull procurement, sire sampling (PGA), and correct semen usage (SMS) are immeasurable.

Select Embryos Inc., was closed and replaced with a smaller program whose main focus was to provide embryos that better fit an international market. A year later, the facilities were revamped to facilitate bull housing and re-named the Hecker Center in dedication to John Hecker and all that he did to help establish a world-class sire program at Select Sires.

It is still the sires and the people that have made Select Sires the preferred provider of dairy and beef genetics across the world. The 1980s and 1990s ushered in some of the all-time greats to share the stalls at Select Sires. Some notable sires available at the time included 7HO1236 Fisher-Place MANDINGO TW, a very popular Excellent (95) son of SWD Valiant that became the first sire ever to produce one million units of semen. 7HO1897 To-Mar BLACKSTAR-ET, an Excellent (93) son of 9HO584 Cal-Clark Board CHAIRMAN may have made more money for producers through high selling daughters and sons than any other sire across the world. Born in 1978, 7HO980 Walkway Chief MARK (VG-87-GM) produced tremendous brood cows and is prevalent on the maternal side of many high-profile families. 7HO543 Carlin-M Ivanhoe BELL (EX-93-GM), born in 1974, was a sire ahead of his time for components and production and is still found as a key sire in the background of many modern sire pedigrees today.

As the Dick Chichester era came to a close on December 31, 1999, the new millennium began with new leadership for the cooperative in the form of David Thorbahn and

Select Sires kept a strong focus on breed-leading sires with an added interest in new services. Talented people can do amazing things and it was only fitting that this new era of Select Sires would invest many resources into helping customers maximize their genetic investment. As farms grew, additional expertise was needed to ensure that the products of Select Sires were being used appropriately. C.E.O. Thorbahn led a charge to have a highly- trained team of experts available for member-owners to implement and use the sires and products Select Sires offered. Programs like Select Mating Service took on new responsibilities and offerings while new programs such as Select Reproductive Solutions were developed to meet the growing focus on reproduction and getting cows pregnant.

Much time and effort was spent to develop a plan on how to best take the expertise to the field and even more effort was spent in executing the plan to its fullest potential. It was a bold step from a company that had outstanding sires and products with minimal services available to becoming a company offering a complete portfolio of products and services that a producer could employ to save time and money. Growing farms had growing responsibilities and a farm manager could no longer manage every aspect of the operation without assistance. Beginning with the new century and continuing until today, countless producers have called on Select Sires as a trusted partner to help manage their herd's genetics, breeding programs and animal health.

Mr. and Mrs. Ronald Hope are joined by Robert Rumler, the executive secretary of the US Holstein Association, Dick Chichester and George Miller in recognizing ELEVATION's contribution to the Holstein breed.

New innovations such as genomics accelerated the need for additional expertise on the farm. It is great to have tools, but having a tool and not knowing how to use it can create more harm than good. Just as a welder might need training with a miter saw, breeders looking to advance the genetic profile of their herds looked to Select Sires for the latest tools and guidance on how to use them. The key steps that Select Sires employed in taking genomics to its membership was to identify the genomic profiles that could best move the genetic makeup of herds forward, work with producers on how to best utilize those genomic profiles, and perhaps most importantly, validate the performance with additional herd analysis and progeny testing. Only when all three aspects of a genomic program are working, can a herd accurately see the return on the investment.

New tools also called for new expertise in making the best use of the innovations. As herds grew, each herd chose to manage their genetics and reproduction program somewhat differently. From the genetics standpoint, some herds chose to intensively manage all of the matings of the herd while other herds looked to simplify the process for matching up genetics. In the case of the latter, the StrataGEN program managed inbreeding on the farm while simplifying the day-to-day actions of mating cattle. StrataGEN was recognized by *Dairy Herd Management* magazine as a top innovation in 2012 for its unique ability to simplify productive cattle matings. StrataGEN used highly-reliable genomic inbreeding data to differentiate bulls in the Select Sires lineup, both proven and genomic young sires, into one of five distinct genetic lines.

Some herds continued to individually mate their herd for the best genetic combination, but choose to simplify things on the reproduction end. For those herds, Select Sires innovated timed-A.I. protocols, developed activity monitoring systems and introduced technician programs that manage the breeding program for the herd owner, saving time and money. *Feedstuffs* magazine recognized Select Sires as the top company for technical expertise in 2004 identifying these innovative programs as a way for the cooperative to help its customers be more productive with the same amount of resources. As the world heads toward 9 billion inhabitants, it will be a similar march towards more productive capacity from the same amount of resources that determines the organizations that will continue to succeed. Select Sires has proven to be one of those organizations.

Select Sires continued to invest on behalf of the member-owners of the cooperative in new technology and genetic offerings. In the five years leading up to the 50th anniversary of the federation of cooperatives, Select Sires offered a variety of cattle activity-tracking software including CowManager®, partnered with River Valley Farm on a first-of-its-kind online sire sampling program, provided a method for maximizing return on the lower-end genetics of a herd with the Breeding to Feeding℠ program and acquired GenerVations Inc. to expand the sire lineup and continue strong market growth in Canada. Select Sires continued to be active in providing new offerings because the customer continues to be active in growing his or her business. The company mission statement lists job No. 1 as "enhancing the productivity and profitability of dairy and beef producers" and Select Sires remains a true partner on the farm in accomplishing that goal.

Fifty years is a milestone very few companies reach. The American A.I. industry once had close to 100 A.I. companies dotting the landscape and offering products to customers across the countryside. As former General Manager Dick Chichester has often stated, "the customer votes with their semen purchases for the suppliers that they would like to see continue to offer products and services to them." The companies that survive are the companies that can be most responsive to the needs of the customer and offer the expertise and assistance that truly helps the profitability and success of the customer. Select Sires has thrived because of a connection to the customer through its member-owners. Just as the customer had a large influence 50 years ago when Select Sires was first formed, today the dairy and beef cattle owners that make up Select Sires are elevated to new heights because of their ability to direct the cooperative and the services that it offers. It is a business model that works.

2

◆ ◆ ◆

Select Sires: Of the People,
By the People and For the People

◆ ◆ ◆

Perhaps the 1970 Select Sires dairy sire directory said it best when it described the five-year-old organization in the following terms: "Select Sires, Inc. located at 1224 Alton-Darby Rd., Columbus, Ohio, has one primary objective in mind and that is to provide dairymen across the country the ultimate in a sire program." It goes on to say, "The organizational structure of Select Sires provides the owner-members the opportunity to continue service within their respective areas and maintain their own individual offices and staff. Their main objective is to provide the utmost in service to their members." The excellent description fills the inside front cover about the fledgling company, its goals for the future and how it plans to accomplish these goals. It cannot be called a "mission statement" because it is much too long in verbiage and goes into too much detail to fit the modern definition of a mission statement, but it did deliver the message loud and clear. Select Sires was serious about becoming a major player in the A.I. industry and it was going to attract the best people in the industry to join the team to get it done.

One chapter in a book cannot do justice to all of the people that have helped Select Sires become successful. Talk to a Select Sires employee, a Select Sires board member or a Select Sires customer and you will quickly hear that for as great as the sire lineup and product offering has been at Select Sires, it is still the people and that personal interaction that makes the difference. This chapter will look at the type of people that have helped to make Select Sires the first choice of cattle breeders around the world for 50 years.

In the dairy industry being called a "cow man"* is quite the compliment. It means that someone has identified that person as a person committed to good cows and how good cows can be made better. Select Sires started out as a semen exchange program that put genetics from one area into another area and is the work of "cow men" and their desire to get the best genetics possible. A semen exchange program does not exist simply to control costs; if costs were the main interest a company would just find the cheapest source and use that source exclusively. A semen exchange program does not exist because it is the easy thing to do; inventories must be managed, semen must be shipped and fair trades must be negotiated. Select Sires came about because "cow men" had an interest in gaining access to and control of the best genetics for use in their herds. Men and women from individual cooperatives had a nice lineup of sires in their own sire listings and saw opportunity in sharing these genetics, managing inbreeding and gaining access to the best sires available. It was a hallmark of Select Sires in 1965 and it remains a focus of Select Sires in 2015.

The term "cow man" includes women as well, we use the more widely recognized gendered industry term here but it really pertains to all people that recognize and appreciate a good cow.

To identify the best genetics, Select Sires formed sire committees for the dairy breeds to discuss the direction that the Select Sires sire department should take. Successful

The attendees of the 1972 Select Sires Sales Conference.

A meeting of the 1976 Holstein Sire Committee meeting

dairy managers that worked closely with their cattle identified the traits that were most important to them and the success of their operations. In the early days, the sire committees actually identified cow families and potential bull mothers that could serve as good brood cows for Select Sires members across the country. Today, the sire committees still exist and take on more of a consultation role working with the Select Sires sire analysts on the type of animal that they want on their farms and in their production environments. It is the consistency and leadership of the ownership of Select Sires that has maintained the focus of the genetic lineups at Select Sires to be in tune with the needs and wants of the customer.

Perhaps the purchase of 7HO58 Round Oak Rag Apple ELEVATION (EX-96-GM) best exemplifies how the people that formed Select Sires worked together in a structure "of the people." ELEVATION was born August 30, 1965 at the farm of Ronald Hope, the cousin of George Miller. A Virginia Tech graduate, George Miller had been employed at Virginia Artificial Breeders Association (VABA) since 1956 and was named manager of VABA in 1965, the same year as ELEVATION's birth. Miller was aware of the bull as he had worked at Round Oak Farm for five years and suggested the mating of Tidy Burke Elevation on a gangly two-year-old at the farm, Round Oak Ivanhoe Eve (EX-94). A bull calf resulted, but as manager, Miller had already informed his board of directors that he would not push sires from Round Oak on them, as it would be a conflict of interest. The Virginia Holstein Field Day was being held at Foxlease Farm in 1966, the same county as Round Oak Farm and a field man for the cooperative and a member of the board knew the members of the sire committee were all present in the county, so they lined up a visit of the committee to go inspect ELEVATION. The VABA sire committee inspected the bull and everyone liked what they saw in the 11-month-old bull. The committee did agree that they wanted to acquire the bull on behalf of VABA but the asking price for ELEVATION was $3,000 and VABA had never paid more than $1,000 for a Virginia-bred young bull. After discussing his merits, the sire committee did approve the purchase of ELEVATION for $3,000. Miller was able to acquire him for $2,800 and the sire that Holstein International named "The Bull of the Century" was in line to join Select Sires thanks to people interested in breeding good cattle working together.

In addition to sire committees, many other committees assist the Select Sires board of directors in providing direction to the management of the cooperative. Two of the newer committees to be formed include the Production Review Committee and the ART Committee. The addition of committees over time reflects the growing need for member input into the direction of the cooperative. The first committees formed to serve the board focused on genetics and facilities management. As new areas of innovation and focus were identified by strategic planning sessions, new committees were formed to address these issues. The "cow man" was still a big part of Select Sires employees and the member leadership of the cooperative, but now "repro person" and "genomics person" were also playing a huge role in setting the course for Select Sires.

In looking at the styles of hiring good people in 1965 compared to 2015, it is notable to mention the contrast and challenges that faced a start-up organization like Select

The sire department team in the 1990's included Lon Peters, Rodger Hoyt, Scott Culbertson, Ron Long, Charlie Will, and Jeff Ziegler.

Bulls are often the photogenic stars of Select Sires but there are always people behind the scenes helping the bulls to shine. Here Dairy Progeny Specialist Jeff Brown works with Jake Hartman, livestock technician and Kari Kronberg, former intern to capture a photo.

Sires in 1965 compared to the recognized industry leader that Select Sires is today. The early years of Select Sires called on leadership from the individual member cooperatives to guide the organization. The first general manager of Select Sires was Jim Mellinger, who joined the organization from COBA where he had been sales and service manager. An early move of the new federation was to consolidate production at a few locations. This prompted two key moves that would set the course for Select Sires moving forward; additional member cooperatives would be needed to capitalize on economies of scale with semen production and that the member cooperatives of Select Sires would have to adjust to being sales and service organizations without the responsibility of bull studs. Contrast this to recent history where Select Sires purchased Sire Power assets in 2000 and GenerVations and Sire Lodge assets in 2014 to garner additional production facilities and protect export capabilities with production facilities in different countries.

From a semen production standpoint, when Select Sires personnel traveled to Europe in 1970 to research the practice of a new plastic straw for freezing semen, it was General Manager Mellinger and Director of Production Howard Kellgren that did the investigating. That would have represented a high percentage of the available manpower at Select Sires at the time. When a new semen production method is investigated today, the resources of Select Sires would allow input from Vice President of Processing and Research Mel DeJarnette, retired Vice President of Processing and Research Clif Marshall (still a part-time employee to Select Sires), Director of Research Matt Utt, Vice President of Technical Programs Dr. Ray Nebel and Western Manager of Technical Services Program King Smith, three on-staff veterinarians and many other trained personnel with an ability to provide constructive feedback on a decision for the membership. The findings are then presented to the Production Review Committee for review and Select Sires can quickly implement new techniques to benefit the end-user, the Select Sires customer. This reflects the power of a cooperative with growth. A key thing to remember with all of these resources is that Select Sires still maintains a focus on producing a product economically for all members without a lot of unnecessary overhead. A competitor once compared modern-day Select Sires to the New York Yankees for the ability to add a key person to the team when needed. This comparison is only partially correct, the New York Yankees have a reputation for adding people with little regard for budget, Select Sires does desire to have the best people on the team but only when the investment will provide a positive return to the member-owners.

After all, it is people that make the difference. There are very few companies where a person with 10 years of service would be considered the "new guy," but a quick review of the years of service at Select Sires and many of the member cooperatives shows that the average years of service is generally between 15 and 20 years of service. Add to that the commitment of the board of directors and delegates that serve Select Sires and the member cooperatives and it is easy to see how the cooperative has maintained a close connection to the membership.

The Select Sires board of directors serves as a close connection between the member-owners utilizing Select Sires on their farms and the management of Select Sires and the member-cooperatives. Each of the board members has a working farm and is keenly

Headquarters staff from 1990 at the Annual Meeting.

The Select Sires Board of Directors joins the newest Select Sires employees at the Sire Lodge facility in Canada.

aware of the needs that Select Sires should be meeting for them. The board identifies these needs and finds the people that can manage the cooperative to best serve the membership. Charles Moellendick was the president of Select Sires board in 1999 when David Thorbahn was hired to replace the retiring Dick Chichester. Charles and his family moved to Ohio in 1971 from West Virginia and operated a dairy farm in Ohio that fit the model for many of the dairies in the area, they began with 75 cows on 400 acres and eventually grew to milk 175 cows in a double-eight parlor with additional acreage. The Moellendick family began working with COBA/Select Sires in 1971 and by 1980 Charles was ready to become more involved in the leadership of the cooperative becoming a member of the COBA/Select Sires and Select Sires board of directors. It was fitting that Charles would be president of Select Sires when the new general manager would be selected to replace Dick Chichester as his father had been president of West Virginia Animal Breeders when Chichester was first hired as the leader of that cooperative.

Charles recalls the selection process as such, "We had four excellent candidates and we had reached a point after the interviews where we needed to discuss our selection. We went around the room and each of the board members had to share what we liked about the candidates. Everyone had to offer their thoughts to the group as it was important to hear all viewpoints and there would be no abstaining from this discussion.

After all of the feedback was shared, the board decided that Thorbahn had the best vision for directing Select Sires. He did not come from a cooperative structure but we were confident that he understood the importance of grassroots input to Select Sires."

Just as Charles Moellendick represented a key constituency of Select Sires core customer during his leadership, current Board of Directors Chairman Myron Czech also represents a growing segment of customers within the cooperative. Myron and his wife Debra operate two dairy farms with their family. The Pike Hills Dairy LLC is a 600-cow purebred Holstein dairy in Little Falls, Minn., and is managed with their daughter Micki, while the 1,300 cow Holstein and Jersey crossbreed herd in Rice, Minn., is managed with their son Brent. The family farms 2,500 acres of corn and alfalfa to help feed the herds. Myron mentions that it was Select Sires' genetics that first got him interested in the cooperative in the mid-1970's and that it is the innovations in technology that is currently a focus for Select Sires that keeps him so enthused. Myron shares, "I became interested in Select Sires for the great sires they advertised. Unfortunately, Select Sires was not routinely available in Minnesota at the time. Thankfully that did not last long and we soon had access to Select Sires when Minnesota joined the Select Sires family in 1986. I was attracted by the sire lineup but what really got me hooked were the people and programs. The greatest bulls in the world can do little good unless they translate into high value pregnancies on our dairy. The Select Reproductive Solutions (SRS) program is the tool that evaluates and guides the team that manages reproduction on our dairy."

As chairman, Myron credits the structure of Select Sires as a key reason for success, "To me the calling card of Select Sires is that they are large and diverse enough to fulfill

Select Sires has always has a strong connection to breed associations. Here, attendees at the 2003 National Jersey Convention enjoy a bull parade.

Seven of the ten people pictured in this photo of the 2000 sire department team are still active at Select Sires fifteen years later. Back row L-R: Lon Peters, Charles Will, Scott Culbertson, Jeff Ziegler, Ron Long, Dave Thorbahn and Rick VerBeek. Front row L-R: Blaine Crosser, Charles Sattler and Jerad Haase.

any need and personal enough through the federated structure to pay attention to the details." Myron and other board members are quick to mention that it is the highest quality people working with a blend of products and services that have allowed Select Sires to grow from humble beginnings to being the current market share leader. Looking to the future, Myron adds, "Appreciation for outstanding products and people is universal. The same qualities that propelled Select Sires to be the current U.S. leader should have the same effect outside the United States as well. Select Sires' reputation for integrity in everything we do has made us a logical first choice for companies wanting to bring new technologies to the marketplace."

The export growth for Select Sires has been very real and yet board policy still states that domestic demand should remain the first focus when production at Select Sires is allocated. One man that has witnessed a lot of this growth in many different roles is Blaine Crosser. Crosser grew up on a registered Guernsey farm in northeast Ohio and joined Select Sires in December of 1977 after graduating from The Ohio State University. He has coordinated international tours, managed daughter photography, prepared sire catalogs, coordinated export shipments and managed international sales. His current position, Dairy Sire Product Manager, means that he is responsible for getting the right semen to the right places. With sales of 15 million units per year, this does present challenges. Crosser shares, "Today my responsibilities center around having the right bulls on collection, in the right barn, with the right amount of inventory to meet sales demand and to get the product distributed to every market in a timely manner." It is another example of people making the difference as Crosser works with barn crews to move animals, sire analysts to estimate demand, production staff to predict total production capabilities and communications staff to develop materials that support the sire on the supply end while working with member cooperatives and the semen order form that has more than 400 different sires available for order on the demand side.

A plaque was dedicated at the 1991 Annual Meeting honoring the charter member directors from 1965.

When asked about the challenges faced from growing from 5 million units of sales at the 25 year anniversary to 15 million units of sales today, Crosser adds, "The biggest challenge from growth centers around having enough product to meet the demand and balancing the needs of the domestic and international markets. As our owners, our members always come first, so finding ways to increase semen production via additional research was necessary to keep up with the growth in our export business. Sexed semen presented another set of challenges to efficiently use the number of sperm cells that our best sires could produce

Sales representatives of Select Sires inspect 7HO6417 O-MAN at a national sales conference.

Members of the Board of Directors for Select Sires move the first shovelfuls of soil for the new building project in 2009 providing two new barns meeting European Union requirements.

to meet the demand for both conventional and sexed semen at the same time. Finally, the most recent challenge has been the market shift to heavier use of high genomic young sires that produce fewer sperm cells and fewer straws than mature proven bulls. With each challenge come new opportunities."

Those opportunities all come back to people and this book will look at how Select Sires' people have listened to the customer and executed a plan for meeting the needs of that customer. As an owner of the cooperative, the Select Sires customer has a unique opportunity to influence the path of the federation. The member-owner at the top of the pyramid selects other member-owners to represent them on the board of directors, committees and delegate bodies that give them a voice. Those leaders select the leadership and management of Select Sires whose job then becomes to strategically plan the direction of the cooperative with guidance from the board. It then becomes the job of over 900 men and women that wear the Select Sires diamond to execute the plan and meet those needs. People do make the difference.

General Manager Dick Chichester being interviewed during a CBS news documentary.

◆ ◆ ◆

An Interview with Dick Chichester

◆ ◆ ◆

At the August 14, 1973 Select Sires board meeting, Richard (Dick) H. L. Chichester was named general manager of Select Sires, a short time after he had been appointed acting general manager following the resignation of Jim Nichols. The steady hand of Chichester's leadership was an excellent follow-up to the leadership of General Manager Nichols, who had helped get Select Sires up and running. Nichols resigned because of some degree of disagreement on the pace at which Select Sires should move and expand. Some of the member cooperatives felt that things were happening too quickly and the measured pace of Chichester's Southern personality was a perfect fit for the events currently occurring within Select Sires.

The following is an interview that occurred in the winter of 2013 with Chichester reviewing the 27 years of his involvement with Select Sires and his recollections and thoughts on the development of North America's largest A.I. organization.

How did your interest in cattle begin?

Chichester: My grandfather was a justice of the Virginia Supreme Court after starting as a Circuit judge. His interest was really in cattle however, and he started a farm of 15 to 20 cows near my boyhood home in Fredericksburg, Va. in 1915. His interest was so strong that he would travel across the east coast to find Guernsey cattle for his breeding program. One of his first big purchases was a Guernsey bull from Mr. Macy, who had started the Macy's department stores. The bull came down from New York on a boxcar and he was walked three miles from the train depot to the farm. This bull turned out to be quite a transmitter and my grandfather's $150 purchase eventually turned into a $20,000 sale in 1919 to Mr. Babson of milking equipment fame. You can imagine that something like that would create my interest in bulls and it stuck!

What were some of your work experiences before Select Sires?

Chichester: I graduated from Virginia Tech and returned to the home farm for a few years. Those years were some of the worst years for drought in my memory and I realized I should probably pursue my main interest of working with bulls. So I sold my cows in 1960 and was offered a job with the West Virginia Breeders Cooperative (a precursor to Sire Power). I accepted the job and convinced my wife to move to West Virginia into a house that came along with the position. My wife got to the kitchen and she just fell to the floor and started crying. It was not a real great place but it was my first opportunity to get working in A.I. I managed the co-op and worked with the 26 technicians in that group, handling mostly fresh semen at that time. I did that for three years and then the merger between West Virginia and Maryland occurred.

In 1963, I moved to Frederick, Md. to head up the bull buying for the partnership of West Virginia and Maryland breeding cooperatives. Previously the cooperative sire committees were responsible for all of the purchases and some ulterior motives on the behalf of some committee members meant that some bulls got into the program that would have been better off not getting into the program. ABS and Curtiss had formalized plans and money. We knew if we were going to keep up with them and do the best job for our members that we needed to have some long-range genetic plans. It became my duty to identify possible sire acquisition and present them to the sire committee for purchase approval. I worked in sire acquisition for the group that became Sire Power until 1971.

In the summer of 1971, Jim Nichols was hired as general manager at Select Sires. I was offered the position of director of public relations and I turned him down. But

Dick Chichester stands with Stan Cameron, Howard Kellgren, and Fred Friday at the building project that would become the Kellgren Center.

Nichols was a great recruiter and he had dairymen and several other people that I respect a lot call me that following week and encourage me to join Select Sires. It was like I was a high school player being solicited for a college football team. That was my entry into Select Sires.

Describe your first few years as general manager at Select Sires:

Chichester: In 1973, Virginia Tech approached Nichols about becoming the dean of the college of agriculture. Obviously that is a tough job to turn down and around the same time, some of the members were rebuffing some of Nichols ideas to expand and consolidate the federation into one entity. The politics of the situation caused Nichols to leave and the board approached me about running the organization until they found somebody qualified. I told them I would do it but I wanted them to get somebody qualified as soon as they could. As it turns out, it was 27 years later until they found somebody qualified!

Right off the bat, some political problems did continue. We had been using COBA's facilities as headquarters and the decision was made that we needed to build our own facilities. Well, when you have to borrow money, each member cooperative has to sign on to take on the debt. Illinois Breeders Cooperative was short on cash and they had real concerns about the long-term effectiveness of the group and they wanted to pull out. In July of 1973, I convinced the Illinois group to meet with me before making any long-term decisions to show them the bright future that Select Sires had and the strong sire and service offerings that would be a hallmark of the cooperative. Unfortunately my father died the day we were to have the meeting. My requests to the Illinois group to reschedule the meeting fell on deaf ears and they made the decision to pull out of the federation.

So a few days after burying my father, I was on a plane to Illinois to try and salvage what could be saved of the Select Sires business in the area. Ray Hess, a former leader of the Illinois Breeders Cooperative, joined me and we went around Illinois talking to technicians and possible employees for the business. A lot of people signed on and we had the Illinois-Wisconsin division of Select Sires up and running. We began to get farmers involved as well and our success continued to grow. Several years went by and the Illinois Breeders Cooperative contacted us about rejoining Select Sires. So we traveled to Chicago to meet with their representatives. After much discussion and thoughtful consideration, the Select Sires board decided to have the Illinois Breeders Cooperative come back into the organization. There were still some hard feelings on both sides so the decision was made to give the new entity a fresh start with a new name. In August of 1979, this group became Prairie State and eastern Iowa was also added to the coverage area of that cooperative.

Michigan was also contemplating pulling out around the same time. I traveled up there and talked to them about the positives of staying with Select Sires and we were able to convince them to stay with Select Sires. Of course, my friends, 7HO58 Round Oak Rag Apple ELEVATION (EX-96-GM) and 7HO91 No-Na-Me Fond MATT (EX-91-GM) were a good help in getting that done.

What are some other memorable moments in building Select Sires?

Chichester: All West Breeders had some history with Select Sires but it had never worked out for them to join the group. In the mid-1970's, Archie Nelson who was a friend of mine from All West, called and said that they were getting some overtures from ABS and that some members of their group were pushing for the group to join ABS. I got on a plane and met Archie in Seattle at the airport and we talked about the possibilities. All West had a strong interest in Select Sires because they had history with us and knew that Select was going to offer the most bull power. Their concern was availability of semen. So we had some customer meetings to discuss the benefits that would happen with All West becoming a member of Select Sires. I always tried to seat myself near the folks that appeared to be the ones against All West

The 1991 Select Sires Annual Meeting was a celebration of 25 years of progress. History book author Bernie Heisner, is presenting a copy of the book to Board President Clarence Boyke and General Manager Dick Chichester.

joining the federation. I specifically remember smoking a cigar with a cigar-smoking objector during a break at one of the meetings. Usually if you could connect with the people and show them that Select Sires had their best interests at heart, you could get things done. So All West did vote to join Select in 1975 and it was a key in continuing our sales success on the west coast. Of course, any time you added a new member, there was also concern from the existing members about giving up semen. We only had a fixed amount of semen production capabilities and a new draw on inventory would have to come from some existing member's pool. The board discussed each case very carefully. They weren't all slam-dunks but at the end of the day the board acted with the best interest of the whole group in mind.

When Dick Kellogg retired from COBA, the East Central Breeders manager Wally Erickson was hired to lead COBA. The best time to add a new member cooperative is when leadership is in transition and I reached out to a well-known breeder, Clarence Boyke, who had just called me about wanting more 7HO195 Wapa Arlinda CONDUCTOR (EX-90-GM) semen. I asked him about East Central joining Select and he said they would look into it. We invited the board to Ohio to see the new facilities and the efficiency of the operation was impressive to them. The board voted in favor of joining Select Sires, so they took it to a membership vote. The day of the meeting I visited some breeders and Clarence and I answered questions from the floor at the meeting that night. The vote for East Central to join Select Sires was almost unanimous. Clarence was one of the best leaders I worked with while at Select Sires and he really moved things forward.

In 1984 (I remember it because it was the day after the presidential election), a competitive group was running roughshod over the Minnesota Valley group and we were approached about meeting with some of the existing employees of Minnesota Valley. After that first meeting, we had about half of the group signed on and we were well on our way to having a new member cooperative. The group quickly got organized, joined Select Sires, and Minnesota Select Sires Co-Op Inc., with their first general manager Lyle Kruse, really grew market share in that region.

Finally in 1999, DuWayne Kutz, the general manager of Sire Power, contacted us and relayed to us that the Sire Power board felt like they did not have the resources or bull power to continue operating as they were. He polled his board to rank all of the competitors that they should talk to about joining and Select Sires came out ranked No. 1. So some discussions occurred but Virginia-North Carolina was actively marketing in Pennsylvania and Maryland. Due to alliances to existing offices and sales arrangements, we just could not get everyone on the same page for making a relationship work at that time. David Thorbahn was able to get the groups assimilated shortly after he began in 2000.

Why has Select Sires been successful?

Chichester: Well, ELEVATION made a rookie manager look good, but from there we have always been fortunate to have a lineup of bulls that were in demand. 7HO477 GLENDELL Arlinda Chief (EX-93-GM), 7HO195 Wapa Arlinda CONDUCTOR (EX-90-GM), 7HO191 WAYNE-Spring Fond Apollo (GP-82-GM)… the list goes on and on, the TPI® dominance has always been there. Success and growth usually go hand-in-hand and World Wide Sires has also been a key to our growth. There was some discussion on how we could best handle our international marketing and Bill Clark from World Wide Sires invited George Miller and me out to Hanford, Calif. to see how our groups could work together. It was pretty obvious that selling semen to World Wide Sires on a wholesale basis for international marketing could work if we made sure that the member cooperatives of Select Sires were taken care of first. That worked out pretty good for both parties. Our member cooperatives got the bulls they need for our member-owners and World Wide Sires could market bulls for us with no additional overhead to our members. In Latin America, we also saw strong growth with Jerry Fickel and his team. Again, it all comes back to people.

Who were some of the key people that you worked with at Select Sires?

Chichester: When I became temporary manager, I needed a marketing manager. My first call was to George Miller. The reason I called George was because he was honest and he would tell you what he really thought. Sometimes people thought we were going to come to blows because George's voice would get raised but he really was just concerned about doing things right.

In our sire directory, we implemented a star program where the sires' traits were ranked by different stars. That system was OK but we really needed a mating service, some program that could match up the best sires to our dairymen's cows. I had worked with a Holstein classifier that really had a good eye for cattle, Ron Long. As I observed his work, I thought he did a good job of scoring cattle and I often agreed with his analysis so I knew we could see eye-to-eye on the breakdowns. More importantly, Ron had a great rapport with herd owners. He could explain how he scored a cow the way he did and he did it as a gentleman without saying negative things. He had returned to Ohio to work on a farm and we had dinner to discuss a new position of a mating leader. I wrote out a job description on a napkin and he went on to become Select Mating Service (SMS) evaluator No. 1. The one thing I insisted on is that the program must be a breed improvement program and not an inventory management program. If the bull fits the cow, we put him in there. Some programs seem designed to use up excess inventory and we did not want that.

When I arrived, our Program for Genetic Advancement young sire program was run by a man that wanted to buy bulls and who also thought that his Ph.D. was worth extra salary. I wasn't highly educated myself so I didn't think that carried much weight. A competitor had employed a Ph.D. so it was becoming fashionable to hire Ph.D.'s to manage the sire departments of major A.I. companies. I have always felt that you end up with better bulls when you listen to the farmer and the customer, so I didn't see the value in having a Ph.D. just to say we have a Ph.D. managing our department. Another competitor wanted to hire this guy from us, and that was just fine with me. It opened the position for Rodger Hoyt.

Rodger was a detail man that was also a perfectionist. He was exactly what we needed to manage our young sire program. He developed a good program, had a lot of follow-up, and put a system in place that could keep track of the growing number of young sires in our program. I believe some of the recording devices developed by Rodger are still in use today.

At that point I also needed to add a marketing person to replace the position I vacated. Bernie Heisner was a natural fit for that job. He had written for Hoard's Dairyman and had a good idea of how to relate the strengths of a sire to the needs of a dairyman. Bernie always had a desire to run something so he left to become the manager of the American Guernsey Association before eventually becoming the General Manager of COBA/Select Sires. After he left for Guernsey, we hired Sue Alderman to do our advertising. Sue was the first woman on staff and she did a great job promoting what we were trying to accomplish.

In the 1970s things were really moving along and we had approximately 1,000 bulls in Ohio. Howard Kellgren, our director of production, came to me and said that we needed a full-time veterinarian on staff. We had been sharing a veterinarian with the Columbus Zoo but with that many bulls I agreed that it was time to add a veterinarian to our staff to take care of these valuable genetics. So we interviewed around and got the No. 1 vet from the vet class at the University of Illinois Vet School, Dr. Don Monke.

Dr. Monke was on top of things and was a perfect fit for the growing number of government entities and regulations that a company like ours had to deal with to sell semen. In fact, we had a few discussions on always doing the right thing but when there is a gray area, let's remember that our customers count on us to sell semen. Especially challenging for Dr. Monke was the cadre of government veterinarians that used to enjoy utilizing the authority that they had been given. Don would get frustrated and I would often remind him that while he was the No. 1 graduate in his class, he now had to deal with the bottom third!

The whole thing revolved around people that knew what they were doing. Finance was another area where we were always fortunate to have good people. Don McKean was one of the first leaders in that department and he came over from COBA at the request of Jim Nichols. Don was bored in a meeting one day and got to doodling, well the diamond doodle that he drew ended up becoming the Select Sires diamond logo that we use today. That logo was there from day one; people often think you need a high-price ad agency to develop these items and that was nothing more than a doodle.

What is the key to the longevity of Select Sires?

Chichester: Longevity is because of dedicated people. I have always said you don't have to fire people if you hire the right people in the first place. The dairy and beef customer doesn't care who the manager is at Select Sires, it is the people on the front line that are the face of Select Sires. The person that calls on them better be the best person that they know of for genetics and reproduction. It all comes down to good *service, good genetics and high conception.*

Our low turnover obviously helps with sales. We have a lot of people that have been connecting with the customer for 20, 30, 40 years. I call it the gate theory. If you have cows on either side of a fence and you open a gate, the cows that feel like the other side is a more attractive place will go through the gate. We have a lot of people that like to walk through the gate to Select Sires. We have a family atmosphere and people feel that Select Sires is home. Treat people the way they should be treated and then offer them a good product to sell and people will be attracted to that situation. We have always had good bulls and that helps a lot. When we moved in to new markets and had to attract new people, it made it easy to get the right people on board.

Do you care to speak a little bit about the Select Sires business model?

Chichester: We always said, "Remember who your customers are. We are not working for each other or a corporate structure, we are working for the benefit of the dairy and beef producer." So we have always had our farmer-owners at the top of the pyramid. Then we had a level of member organizations in the middle coordinating with Select Sires on what we need to offer. It has worked well but we also had to remember, "a camel is a cow that was put together by a committee." By saying that I mean that you do have to find the right people to be in leadership positions and then count on them to make the right decisions. That holds true for our board of directors, member employees and the Select Sires staff.

Select Sires has always been at the top of the list for great bulls. What do you attribute that to?

Chichester: To answer that I'll look at the new genomic lists. Genomics came into play long after I retired but I was talking with some of our sire analysts and asked them why we have done so well in acquiring those types of bulls as well. Their answer reinforces what we have already talked about and that is the relationships that we have with our customers. The relationships built long ago helps to get the best bulls to Select Sires. All things being equal, breeders would rather have that bull at Select Sires because of the solid foundation and the soundness of the organization.

We had to work for that trust. In the early 1970s, before ELEVATION was really doing big things, we bought young bulls and we made the first payment when the bulls were acquired and then we gave the second payment when the bull started producing semen. We didn't always have the funds for that second payment readily available but we told the farmer that you would get paid and in the meantime we *will pay you interest on what we owe you. Not everyone was doing that and it really built a level of trust. Some companies would cull a bull without telling a farmer and other competitors would play games with their lineups to please certain providers. We always felt that we need to communicate with our seed stock providers to treat all sides fairly.*

The team of sire analysts at Select Sires today reflects the growth that Select Sires has had in the industry. John Hecker was in charge of the bull buying at Select Sires and we had grown to a level where he just could not keep up with all of the acquisitions we needed to make to have the bull numbers we needed. So we hired someone to assist John and that person was Charlie Will. Charlie was a salesperson in Wisconsin and John hired Charlie to start covering additional parts of the country. Charlie has respect the world over for finding good genetics that producers want to populate in their herds.

An example of that is 7HO1897 To-Mar BLACKSTAR-ET (EX-93-GM). Charlie was at the Tompkins herd in Iowa and knew they had a good WAYNE daughter. This was before the cow family was really well known. He asked to look at the cow and he really liked her. He asked about getting some sons from the cow and it turns out she had a son that was just born, that was BLACKSTAR and the rest is history as far as he goes. That is still part of the art of bull buying. Before computers, our sire analysts had to have perseverance to search out the good ones. Today the information available will tell you where the good ones are at, but a sire analyst must still know the kind of good cows that a Select Sires customer expects to receive.

How has the industry changed in your opinion?

Chichester: In some ways it has changed and in many ways it has stayed the same. I will give you an example using ELEVATION. Virginia Artificial Breeders had bought the bull and they had an agreement with Maryland-West Virginia Breeders to exchange some semen on some young bulls to expand the amount of genetics available to each customer. It would also help in sampling the bulls and the agreement was that if a bull made it, the owning stud would get 70 percent of the semen and the cooperating stud would get 30 percent. ELEVATION was one of those bulls and obviously he had a long period where he was the most in-demand bull in the world. Well, it made some of the Select Sires members upset because there wasn't enough semen to go around but it was a sign of cooperation that we can accomplish more by working together.

Twelve to thirteen years later ELEVATION goes down and the vets checked him out and it was obvious that he wasn't going to get back up. I went back to the pen to see him and I cried. Even in his condition the bull tried to get up because he was that kind of bull, but it was evident that we needed to put him down and we did. I then told the crew to dig a hole out front and we would bury him with a headstone. The crew said that we couldn't do that because the health department won't allow it. I said it is ELEVATION and we are going to do it, if the health department doesn't like it, they can come and dig him back up. Well, he is still out there today along with four others but we did stop burying foundation bulls, the board said we don't want the place to start looking like a graveyard!

What do you see for the next 50 years of Select Sires?

Chichester: Well, the amazing thing is how Select Sires has grown and the course that it is on. When we charted the course, we didn't really design it this way but you look back on the course and it ended up pretty good. That is because we had good people. Genomics came along after I retired, but information changes so rapidly today. A bull can be the hot thing for six months and then he is soon outdated. I was working with a sale committee recently and we were five months out from the sale. I asked the rest of the crew how many calves we had lined up and the response was that we didn't have any because the information changes and we didn't want to line them up too early. That makes planning tough. It really is something that must be managed and watched intently.

The Aggressive Reproductive Technology^{TM} (ART^{TM}) program to me is very interesting. Jeff Ziegler, who manages that program, was an intern for us. He devotes most of his days to looking at pedigrees and genetics then figuring out how the customer of Select Sires is most going to benefit. It is quite a challenge but it is programs like ART that will make our breeders successful. That is an example of a difference in management styles in developing that program. I would have probably not been as anxious to invest in a program like that but Dave saw the value and has embraced the positives of what can happen.

The thing we focus on really hasn't changed in 50 years. We want to offer the best bulls in the industry and we want the best people in the industry to help our breeders have success with them.

• • •

The Future Delivered

• • •

In his 1937 classic book on animal genetics, "Animal Breeding Plans," Jay L. Lush laid the groundwork for the cooperative structure that the leaders of Select Sires followed when establishing the federation. Perhaps the most important data that came from the book and what Select Sires adopted was the understanding that "a primary objective of a bull circle is to get bull service at lower cost, or better bull service at the same cost," but that misidentification of animals (greater than 13 percent at the time of his writing even when animals are recorded at two months of age) can derail any analysis of which bulls should continue to be used and which "bulls should go to the butcher."

The ability to properly distribute semen to be used, to accurately record how the semen is used, and to track the performance of resulting offspring is crucial to any progeny test program. The leaders of Select Sires Program for Genetic Advancement (PGA) understood this and took great care in investing in and setting up the program for success. It has been an example of a cooperative principle of cooperation, research and return.

The early leadership of Select Sires understood that any patron choosing to use Select Sires is doing so to make an investment in better cattle for his farm. Initially this meant identifying the cows that were most productive in order to produce offspring that could

Rodger Hoyt visits with a patron of COBA Select Sires on the performance of the PGA daughters in his herd.

be produced with a planned mating to be more productive than the parents. With limited production data and no genomic data available in the early stages of Select Sires, the original method for selecting sires happened at the most local level. Sire committees would be aware of the best cattle in their area, the committee would share that information with the group, and the group would then make a decision about whether the genetics of the identified individual would be worth reproducing in other farms in the area. It was a good method but even early members of the sire committee realized that a different environment required a different kind of cow, a different facility required a different kind of cow, different feedstuffs required a different kind of cow, and so on. The decision was made that if Select Sires was truly going to be a national leader in bovine genetics, then the organization also needed to implement a progeny-testing program that would represent all of the membership with a random use of young sire semen. It was a bold decision as the course they were about to chart was not the simplest method and it definitely was not the most economical method; it just was the right method.

Thus, the groundwork was laid for a sampling system that would have capacity for sampling in herds of all different sizes, in all types of facilities, in differing environments and geographies, and with other management treatments that could affect the perfor-

The Rodger Hoyt PGA Facility serves as the main sire-in-waiting facility for Select Sires. Originally called the Darby Creek Facility, it has doubled in size from its original eight barns.

mance of an animal considered so that the resulting progeny data would be as accurate as possible. It is a hallmark of the PGA that continues until this day. Ask any genetic expert why Select Sires has continually dominated the Top 100 TPI sire list at 97 percent reliability and they will point to the sampling methods of the PGA as the reason why. Without the diversification in sampling, a sire could win the "testing lottery" and get sampled in a production environment that suits his offspring perfectly. Unfortunately as progeny numbers grow and more information enters the data, that localized advantage will quickly evaporate. If a genetics provider desires to market semen in many different environments and many different management styles, it must prove its semen works in many different environments and many different management styles. Select Sires' PGA does that work.

When the Program for Genetic Advancement was so named in 1974, Select Sires had already begun to collectively purchase and sample young sires through the member cooperatives in a program informally labeled "Planned Parenthood." The member co-operatives that joined Select Sires had established breeding programs of their own and they brought their best sires with them into the larger lineup of Select Sires. As the formalized bull acquisition program got started at Select Sires with a goal of purchasing the best bulls for the group, the PGA became a key part of ensuring that the goals of the sire program and the actual results being seen on the farm were in step with each other.

A quote that has been much overused at this point but is very relevant in this case comes from the great hockey player Wayne Gretzky. Long considered the greatest hockey player ever to skate, Gretzky was asked the secret to his success and he simply stated, "I don't skate to where the puck is, I skate to where it is going to be." The sire department at Select Sires has always performed thorough research to what dairy and beef breeders want in their herds, the PGA program for dairy sires confirms that the results are being attained.

Since the Program for Genetic Advancement became a formalized program, two industry leaders have managed the program, Rodger Hoyt and Chuck Sattler. Both men had a strong genetic background to go along with strong analytical skills to ensure that the correct information is being recorded and analyzed. Chuck Sattler grew up on a Guernsey farm in Wisconsin and received advanced degrees from the University of Wisconsin in animal genetics and breeding. He spent twelve years working for the National Association of Animal Breeders before joining Select Sires in the year 2000.

One would think that a program for best recording and analyzing data would remain consistent and never have to change. The evolution of milk recording, new milking systems and more flexibility in testing plans means that the PGA has had to change along with the herds that it serves. Add to that the changes by breed associations in the way they collect, compile and publish data and you have a dynamic sampling program constantly adjusting to meet the needs of the current customer while still desiring to offer the best future animal. It calls for new programs that address the new methods and sizes of today's animal agriculture.

The PGA Elite program was introduced in 2008 to meet the need of the growing dairy market. Previously PGA credits were paid on a smaller level when the heifer calf was born and on a greater scale when that animal entered the milking herd. PGA Elite introduced a payment structure that provided most of the sampling incentive up front at time of usage. It allowed Select Sires to capture a large portion of the herds that had expressed a desire to enter the PGA but were unable to previously join due to size restrictions or a need for incentive. PGA Elite meshed the needs of Select Sires and the dairy market place. Select Sires needed additional sampling capacity to move more units for domestic and international marketing while the growing herd size in the U.S. needed additional units from the industry's leading progeny test program. PGA Elite gave the boost that both needed.

As Select Sires looks to the future, there are many opportunities that lie on the horizon. One opportunity is the increased demand for Jersey genetics. The "Jersey Revolution™" has increased demand for Jersey semen in many parts of the world. Select Sires continues to invest in meeting this demand. In 2000, Select Sires sampled 30 Jersey sires, and in 2014 there were 60 Jersey sires being sampled with plans for additional capacity. Genomics helps hone in on the correct sires to bring into the program but there are still limits to the amount of semen that a bull can produce. Future projections for demand mean that additional Jersey sires will have to join the program.

One step that was taken in 2014 to assist the growing demand for Jersey semen was a partnership with River Valley Farm to allow Select Sires customers additional access to some of the top Jersey cattle in the world. River Valley Farm and their focused In Vitro Fertilization (IVF) program for generating high-ranking Jersey offspring produce sire lines that match up with the Jersey needs of Select Sires' membership. A unique online ordering system allows customers to purchase 7JE5000 series sires for use on their own Jersey cattle. The partnership provides additional access and selections for the quickly growing breed through Select Sires' Jersey Revolution.

Another point of focus for the PGA will be the cost effectiveness of gathering data. Production and type data has long been the building block of presenting useful information to cattle breeders selecting genetics to populate their herd. Select Sires has a firm understanding of the economics of the dairy and beef markets and continues to strive to control costs and offer a product that provides real return to the member-owner. The cooperative also has a responsibility to the member to educate and encourage the use of additional cost-effective collection methods within the industry. As parlors and robotic milkers get smarter and are able to collect more information, the recording of data can and should become more automated.

Another future consideration is the value of progeny testing. Select Sires considers progeny testing to be important because there will always be a bottom half of the genetic lineup. Even as that list is pared down using genomic testing, there will still be a top half and a bottom half. Proving that real information in a timely manner helps to provide usable data to the customer quickly through progeny testing. An example is Sire Conception Rate (SCR). Progeny testing allows the sires at Select Sires to get an SCR right off the bat. This gives customers one more tool to use when selecting sires for their program and gives additional insight to the production team at Select Sires as to the actual performance of the bull.

As Select Sires looks to the future, new traits will emerge. Some of these traits will be measured because new technologies now allow the industry to track them with rumination and temperature monitoring. Other traits will be measured because the consumer of the end product will demand new criteria of production either for nutrition or animal care standards. Some of these traits will include foot health, feed efficiency, body temperature and milk flow.

Foot health has always been an important component of a healthy cow. An animal that struggles with mobility or an animal that is frequently lying on the hoof trimmers

In a picture often used in meeting presentations, a young sire in waiting by the name of Ensenada Taboo Planet forecasted a photo filled future with his appearance second from the right in this group of young sires.

table cannot focus on her own health or production. By recording specific actions that were taken on the foot and connecting that to the genetic makeup of the animal, Select Sires can identify the sire lines that are best producing a quality foot and leg to enhance mobility.

Feed efficiency is another trait that has always been considered important, but the dairy and beef industries had limited equipment to track performance of specific genetic lines. Today with beef chutes and milking parlors getting "smarter," the ability exists to measure body weight daily and compare that to the feed consumed. By comparing the feed efficiency of individual animals or groups of animals to the genetic makeup of the animal, Select Sires can produce sires that maximize efficiency at the farm level. With 9 billion worldwide consumers by 2050 looking for dairy and beef in their diet, feed efficiency improvement will allow Select Sires to maximize production with limited resources. FeedPRO® is an important first step in being a proactive cooperative towards meeting these goals.

FeedPRO was introduced in 2009 as an index designed to optimize selection for increasing production and moderating body size while maintaining body condition score and daughter fertility. It was a response to the requests of customers to find a solution to the market challenges they were facing with high feed costs and low milk prices. Research by Select Sires that built on research from the United Kingdom provided a proprietary formula for identifying sires that maximize income over feed costs while also using production, body size traits and other information to produce cattle that are metabolically healthy. University researchers including Maurice Eastridge, Ph.D., of The Ohio State University and Chad Dechow, Ph.D., of Penn State validated the research and sires qualifying for the index are designated with a FeedPRO logo. The decision to work to develop FeedPRO also serves as an example where the proactive nature of Select Sires can provide a genetic advantage to the membership.

The November 2014 edition of *National Geographic* magazine and their article, "The Carnivore's Dilemma" examined the role of animal agriculture in feeding a growing planet and also the impact on natural resources that animal agriculture can provide. Their data shows that cattle, especially beef cattle, can consume up to three times the amount of resources to produce 1,000 consumable calories compared to other animal species and their inefficiencies in production causes a higher proportion of nutrients coming out the other end as well. The article concludes that genetics will be a key answer to the question of increased efficiency in cattle. Just another example of input from the customer providing a head start to Select Sires in identifying the traits that will be most in demand in the future.

Measuring body temperature is another trait that has been enhanced by technology and will also carry additional weight in climates that need heat tolerant genetics. Now that on-cow measuring can produce real-time data as to her temperature and rumination, a producer knowing the baseline for an individual cow and a group of cows can accurately circumvent metabolic disorders that may have needed treatment after clinical signs in the past. The added advantage of identifying sire lines that can best monitor internal temperatures also gives Select Sires a read on the genetics that can work best in warmer environments.

Finally, the total measurement of milk flow will be important in maximizing production with limited resources at the farm. The investment in a robotic milking system or a new parlor is an investment designed to last for multiple years. With the capital expenditure in place, it becomes increasingly important to maximize "milk flow" from the system. Today's new milking technology can accurately measure milk output per cow and give a report on which sire lines are producing the most milk per unit of time. Milk flow is more than just milking speed, it also takes into account the rate at which the animal presents herself to be milked as well as the ability to produce milk in a clean, healthy manner. If a cow is off-production or needs additional intervention for treatment that slows down milk flow, Select Sires can identify the genetics that best serve its member-owner.

The reasons for having an effective progeny test program are very similar in 2015 to what they were in 1965, collecting accurate data validating the performance of genetics in use in the marketplace. As additional data can be recorded and measured, additional selection criteria are established to allow the end user of the genetics to make more accurate decisions. A hungry world is calling for additional product from limited resources. There also is an expectation from that hungry world that the product will be produced in a safe, efficient and humane manner. The Program for Genetic Advancement identifies the sire lines and genetics that can best serve the needs of the consumer in a timely manner.

4

◆ ◆ ◆

The Beginning of Value Added

◆ ◆ ◆

As Select Sires continued to build on the popularity of their early sires and service, the decision was made that more services should be provided to help customers get the most value out of each investment with the cooperative. Today this would be called "value-added," but when Select Mating Service (SMS) was added it was just called a good cooperative principle.

The true value of SMS lies in the realization that the program has transitioned in the value that it has delivered over the years. It began as a simple mating program where evaluators would look at cattle and mate the cattle to the sires best positioned to provide an improvement in ensuing offspring. While still providing that core benefit today, the program has become an all-encompassing vehicle to deliver a whole herd genetic business plan. The mating is still there but it has been joined by inbreeding management, the ability to deliver consistent results across the makeup of the herd and the ability to analyze the performance of the herd and its production. Lon Peters, director of the Select Mating Service program, even likes to compare the program to a "skid loader." He states, "The skid loader does things in a very compact, powerful and efficient manner that other tools on the farm cannot. One size does not fit all with this tool and with a wide range of attachments; the skid loader gets the work done with an ability to cover a wide

The first group gathered at the Select Mating Service conference to listen to analysis from Ron Long. The conference led to a program that now includes over 90 full time evaluators and mates 5 million cattle annually.

array of jobs. The SMS program provides the same kind of hard work and adaptability."

One thing that has not changed is the focus of the program to deliver cattle that suited the dairy owner. Ron Long, former Select Sires evaluator No. 1 says it best when he mentions, "The goal of the program was to focus on the genetics and mating that the customer needed not what we thought they needed." It is a commitment to balanced breeding that rings true today.

In the early days when the mating evaluations were still done on paper and utilized the limited sire data that was accumulated and calculated, the main traits that could be mated to were milk production, fat percent and predicted difference for type. Many of the type traits evaluated today were listed but limited data and limited understanding of the data slowed the ability for rapid improvement. It was here where the SMS program actually helped to fuel its own growth and efficiency. As evaluators saw offspring of some of the sires that were just becoming available for use, they could return reports to the home base and other evaluators so that a better understanding of the sires in use could be made.

It is summed up well in the 1973 Annual Report of Select Sires, the time when the Select Mating Service was just beginning. "Since this segment of the dairy department is relatively new, this report will contain more of the plans for the future, rather than

In 2013, All West Select Sires hosted the SMS evaluators conference. The conference is an annual gathering to exchange ideas and ensure that Select Mating Service personnel are consistent in offering services to Select Sires customers.

what has happened in the year 1973," said Long. "With the increased concern for good functional type of high-producing cattle by our dairymen, it was the feeling of management that Select Sires should put more effort into the area of herd consultation and type evaluation of daughters of bulls coming through our young sire program."

The report then laid out the groundwork for how that would happen. In the area of herd consultation, the paragraph from 1973 feels like it could have been written in 2015. It mentioned that dairymen have been seeking a more efficient cow, knowledge of what is needed to make cows live longer and breeding cattle that do not leave the herd because of physical weaknesses. It then acknowledged that many errors that occur in the use of semen result from a lack of information and lack of knowledge of what a bull could do in the conditions that the cow lived in at the time. The differing conditions of dairy farms became one of the guiding purposes of SMS. "A positive, personalized program of assistance to dairymen, both grade and registered, with the basic purpose to increase the rate of genetic improvement and profit of the herd," said Long.

The standard operating procedures of the new program gave guidance to spell out the work schedule for the SMS consultant:

1. Discuss with the herd owner's plans for the future.
2. Collect data about the herd, including an individual cow analysis.
3. Evaluate the data.
4. Prepare and return to the owner a list of first and second choice matings for each cow, along with other information relative to the breeding program.

The guidance for SMS consultants then finished with an important precept that is still followed today, "The consultant will work with the dairyman and offer his professional advice on sire selection. He will not attempt to dictate bulls to use."

A big addition to the program that helped the efficiency of the evaluator was the movement to computer-based matings in 1983. Steve Moff has been an evaluator for COBA/Select Sires Inc. for 34 years and witnessed most of the innovations to the SMS program. "When we talked about going to a computer mating program, I thought I might lose my job. Jim Lucas and I talked with Rex Castle about how we could do this and we encouraged Ron Long to pursue the idea. There was some resistance but Jim, Ron and I spent several weeks working through the thought process that we use to mate each cow by hand with paper and pencil. We gave our findings to Rex and several weeks later he brought a stack of computer paper two feet high to our office and told us this is the program. That began the process of computer-assisted matings. We began by sending our sheets to the office for processing, then we used data collectors that were finicky depending on the tightness of the hardware, we transitioned to a portable computer that weighed 60 pounds, and eventually ended up with the laptops and handheld data collectors that we use today."

A final responsibility of the consultant was to evaluate young sire daughters for the still unnamed young sire program. It was evident that it was extremely important to know the type transmitting abilities of the young sires to go along with the production data being published. Feedback that came back to Select Sires could be collected and published and offered an additional added value to these sires as they entered the proven sire lineup. Eventually, breed organizations would tackle this responsibility and formalize the program for evaluating young sire daughters, however there still was a large advantage to having the good cow people out in the field evaluate cattle and share their findings with the cooperative.

This tradition of sharing knowledge continues today in the form of an annual SMS consultant's conference. Consultants from across the country and across the globe gather in different regions each year to see different cattle, learn about new programs that can enhance their performance and share observations of sire daughter groups they have been seeing. The sales on many bulls have been affected by the feedback of this group. A review of sales shortly after the evaluator's conference can give a quick read into which sires were liked and which sires were not liked on the tour. Interestingly, it usually does not take long for the actual genetic evaluation of a bull to coincide with the early analysis of this highly-trained and highly-talented group of consultants.

An advantage of the consultant's conference is to quickly and efficiently see daughters of a new bull in a short period of time. David Sarbacker has been evaluating cattle in Wisconsin for East Central/Select Sires for 14 years and had the following comments after a gathering in Michigan; "The farm tours take us to varied herd sizes from the likes of Long Haven to Green Meadow Farms and many in between. This allowed us to see a large number of daughters of bulls from second-crop daughters to new lineup

Steve Moff uses a handheld data collector to score cows for the Select Mating Service.

bull daughters as well as daughters of sires-in-waiting. Seeing second-crop daughters of bulls like 7HO9222 Lincoln-Hill SHOT Laser-ET (EX-92), 7HO9357 Bremer Allegro MAXUM-ET, 7HO9420 Fustead Goldwyn GUTHRIE-ET (EX-94) and 7HO10920 Mr Chassity GOLD CHIP-ET (EX-92) helps me to better utilize these sires and their off-spring in my herds."

The tours also allow evaluators in areas without a traditional PGA young sire base to see the results of the program. After the conference in Michigan, evaluators from Select Sires GenerVations, Frederic Fillion and Stephane Tardif of Quebec added their observations; "We had the opportunity to visit 14 farms of different sizes and breeding philosophies, from 60-cow tie stalls to 3,700 cow free stall operations. Daughters of 7HO10356 De-Su WATSON (EX-90-GM), 7HO9420 Fustead Goldwyn GUTHRIE-ET (EX-94) and others really attracted attention and we realize that we need to use more 7HO8081 Ensenada Taboo PLANET-ET (EX-90-GM) blood in our herds." The investment in the evaluator's conference is substantial but it is an investment that provides a return to the member-owners of Select Sires, with each conference allowing more than 90 "cow people" to get an education about the ability of the sires and programs that are working in cooperator herds.

In 2014, this group of "cow people" analyzed over 5 million cattle in herds utilizing Select Sires. That is quite a pattern of growth from the first year when 9,000 cows were evaluated. What was at one time a pencil and paper job of recording strengths and weaknesses on cows and matching them up to the sires available at the time, has transitioned to a sophisticated computer method of recording pedigree information, scoring the cattle on their type traits and then providing recommended mating sires that offer maximum improvement. With the first two criteria from that list entered, the mating results become very customizable for the customer. Is a Gender SELECTed™ unit desired on this animal? It is easy to adjust. Is a certain price range desired for the third choice on this set of animals? Say it and it is so. It is one more way the original cooperative principles providing what the customer needs comes through in the programs offered by Select Sires.

The use of the service even ensures a patron of the cooperative not participating in the Select Mating Service benefits from the work of the evaluators and managers of the program. The SMS program has always had inbreeding management as a consideration. Where available, the maternal pedigree information is recorded and that information is used to provide mating decisions that offer the introduction of new productive genes to the pedigree. As member herd sizes grew, it was becoming evident that the growing herds still had a desire for many of the benefits of a mating plan but did not have the right arrangement on the farm to implement a plan. Work began on developing a system that could be implemented on a farm with limited labor resources but met the recurring desire to avoid a high level of inbreeding. The StrataGEN program was born.

StrataGEN is an example of how a cooperative can be innovative for the member-own-

Handheld devices used by SMS evaluators have changed quite a bit over the years, consistently offering additional features and services to members of Select Sires.

The professional evaluators of Select Sires are consistent in their results thanks to training events that confirm their mating recommendations best serve the customer.

ers that it serves. Members have a say in the programs that they need to be efficient and as the herd sizes of members grew within Select Sires, some realized that they no longer had an efficient means for implementing SMS matings in their herds. In some cases, the location of the animals made it difficult to use individual corrective matings, in other cases the person performing the insemination did not yet have the ability to match up each breeding to each animal correctly when 100 inseminations were being performed daily. The StrataGEN program allows the herd manager to implement an inbreeding management strategy by rotating breeding lines throughout a herd.

By selecting a color symbolizing different breeding lines prevalent within the Holstein population, a herd manager can take simple steps to avoid inbreeding by using a different color on the animal being inseminated than the color in her parentage. If parentage is known, an ear tag clip or other marking tool can identify the line represented in the animal. If the color of parentage is not known, the color cycle can begin with any line and rotate from there on out. The key is to always use a different breeding line. The system is not perfect and obviously it does not attain the same results that a corrective linear mating program like Select Mating Service can achieve. It does capitalize on what is known about some of the popular breeding lines of today and combines that conformation and production prediction with the genetic profile of the line to avoid inbreeding and deliver a more productive animal than a random mating would produce.

Brad Meek has been mating cows for Select Sires MidAmerica for 15 years and sees innovations such as StrataGEN and the "sire fit analysis" as new tools that help his customers. "My average size mating herd is 500 cows," said Meek. "Using sire fit analysis, I now have the ability to look at the genetic makeup of the herd and quickly identify sires that are a good match for low inbreeding percentage and functional trait fit. I also do Select Reproductive Solutions work, so I can wrap the entire herd program together in one useful tool for the dairy manager." These "new attachments" for the skid steer loader have expanded the reach of the program.

Ultimately the goal remains to produce an animal better than one would achieve with a random mating. The growth of the program would attest to the success that Select Sires customers are seeing in their herds. In 1973, the SMS program began with three part-time evaluators mating 5,800 cows and the introduction of computer mating allowed evaluators to score 225,000 cows in 2,700 herds by 1983. The usage of linear evaluation also grew with the program and this allowed linear blocks to appear in the sire directory in 1984. The benchmark of 500,000 cattle mated annually was achieved for the first time in 1988.

A new option was added to the program in 1991 with the SMS II program that allowed for pedigree mating, a great option for heifers and those farms whose main focus was inbreeding avoidance. In 1993 we saw the benchmark of 1 million cattle mated annually and it was obvious that the program was going to grow exponentially. Additional benchmarks were achieved in 2000 with 2 million matings and 2008 with 4 million matings annually. The program continues to hit new thresholds as SMS evaluators have performed over 5 million annual matings worldwide every year since 2011 with 1.5 million new animals joining the program each year.

In 2011 we also saw the introduction of some popular options to the SMS program with evaluators able to provide genetic rankings of the herd to Select Sires customers as well as sire selection ranking and genomic importation. These tools provided even more information on which to select service sires and allowed Select Sires member-owners to determine which animals from their herd deserved the most attention for creating seedstock and which animals may maximize return to the farm in other roles. This level of expert analysis within the SMS evaluator team provides the opportunity for new programs to be implemented within the cooperative that can serve members such as the Breeding to Feeding program. Utilizing the genetic ranking tools within the SMS program, an evaluator can consult which groups of animals provide the best return for a dairy farm

Angie Kennedy, SMS evaluator for All West Select Sires, evaluating cattle in California

in producing replacements and dairy products while also identifying those animals that provide maximum return to the dairy farm with beef products. It is an inventory management tool again operating with the best needs of the member-owner in mind.

This compilation of additional services introduced as part of the movement towards having a "genetic business plan" in the new millennium added real value to the member-owners of Select Sires. In the early days of SMS, the value of the program was information that the evaluator could provide. There was no "World Wide Web" providing an analysis of what each sire could offer to a dairy, so the evaluator became that conduit for delivering the information to the farm. As time marched on and information became more readily available, the role of the evaluator transitioned from a role of information provider to a consultant. An evaluator had to look at the entire scope of the herd and the goals of the herd owner to provide an analysis of the information and the decisions that the herd owner could make to capitalize on the information. This was a preemptive move by Select Sires and the SMS program to stay relevant to the needs of the customer. Ask any unemployed travel agent what happens when information becomes readily available and he will tell you that your business model must change to stay relevant. The SMS program has remained relevant and has grown by reinventing itself as a program that can manage more than just individual matings.

Peter Matousek, a 23-year evaluator with Select Sires MidAmerica reinforces this concept and mentions that he likes to go by the term that Lon has coined, "genetic consultant." Peter grew up in rural New York and developed an interest in dairy from working on local farms. From there he ended up with a degree in dairy science from the University of Wyoming and went on to manage Arlinda Holsteins in California before joining Select Sires. The herds that he calls on today range from 80 to 12,000 cows but his average herd size has grown to just about 1,000. He mentions, "We have always given genetic advice and that hasn't changed, it is just that today we give that genetic advice along with a discussion on which program will fit the farm the best. My passion is still in seeing cattle improve and how we can make better cattle."

The ability to identify the highest and lowest ranked animals on the farm, tools for animal inventory management and techniques for maximizing the return on a unit of semen within the herd are just a few of the additional services that a modern day SMS evaluator will provide. As time goes on and additional needs arise on the farm, Select Mating Service will continue to adapt the genetic business plan of the farm to meet the goals of the herd owner. Lon Peters has often compared the SMS program to a GPS navigation system providing direction to someone at the wheel of a vehicle. "A GPS device is a small piece of technology that takes information on where I want to be and gives me clear, precise directions on getting me to my destination," said Peters. "The GPS device mirrors the goal of the SMS program in providing time savings for our dairy producers and setting a clear direction for everyday use." Over 5 million matings show that the SMS program is a trusted partner in genetic guidance for the Select Sires member-owners.

◆ ◆ ◆

5

Impact Dairy Sires

◆ ◆ ◆

The advantage that the history of high impact sires at Select Sires has provided to the cooperative is that virtually every dairy farm in the United States and most dairy farms around the world have been impacted by a Select Sires bull. Even to those farms that have never used a unit of Select Sires semen, the Select Sires influence on the genes of the dairy breed populations has been far greater than any other genetic provider. August 2014 data provided by Dairy Agenda Today showed that 53 percent of the elite genomic tested females were sired by Select Sires bulls. Holstein USA published data in 2014 that Select Sires great 7HO58 Round Oak Rag Apple ELEVATION (EX-96-GM) still has more genes present in the Holstein breed than any other bull. The accolades go on and on but the point is that Select Sires has always delivered the type of sire that customers want to use to populate the genetics of their herd.

The early days of Select Sires created a cooperative business model that still exists today. Breeders can pool their resources to acquire the best sires and collectively prove that the expected results are real. The 25 year history of Select Sires covered some of these genetic giants with names that still resonate with dairy breeders; 7HO58 Round Oak Rag Apple ELEVATION (EX-96-GM), 7HO91 No Na Me Fond MATT, 7HO477 GLENDELL Arlinda Chief (EX-93-GM), 7HO401 MARShfield Elevation Tony

Sire Analyst Charlie Will poses with two of the greats of the breed that he acquired, 7HO6417 O-Bee Manfred Justice (OMAN) and 7HO5708 Fustead Emory BLITZ. L-R: Jeremiah Dingledine, Charlie Will and Brian Spires.

(VG-88-GM), 7HO900 Straight-Pine Elevation PETE (EX-90-GM), 7HO543 Carlin-M Ivanhoe BELL *CV (EX-93-GM), 7HO980 Walkway Chief MARK (VG-87-GM), 7HO1118 Arlinda ROTATE (EX-92-GM), 7JE177 Highland Magic DUNCAN and others were recognized for their contribution and impact on the dairy breeds across the nation and around the world. The 25 years that followed have delivered their own impact sires that elicit powerful responses from breeders that were able to move their herds forward with these potent genetics. Present day members of the sire department at Select Sires have shared their thoughts on these impact sires.

The 1985 sire analyst team at Select Sires; Back – Ron Long, Charlie Will, Rodger Hoyt; Front – Scott Johnson and John Hecker

7HO1897 To-Mar BLACKSTAR-ET (EX-93-GM)

BLACKSTAR was sired by the No. 1 TPI sire of the time, 9HO584 Cal-Clark Board CHAIRMAN (VG-88-GM), a sire known for siring great type with fancy udders, making him a natural mating at the time on BLACKSTAR's dam, To-Mar Wayne Hay (EX-90-GMD-DOM).

7HO1897 To-Mar BLACKSTAR

Hay was very typical of the pattern of her sire, 7HO191 WAYNE-Spring Fond Apollo (GP-82-GM), she was big, strong and black, not real stylish, but milked from her great dairy strength. WAYNE also turned out to be a carrier of an undesirable recessive gene called mule foot. Hay had a 50 percent chance of being a carrier, leaving BLACKSTAR a 25 percent chance of being a carrier, Wayne Hay needed to be mule foot tested to be sure BLACKSTAR was not a carrier. Since there was no simple DNA test at the time for mule foot, Wayne Hay had to be flushed from semen from an actual mule foot bull, and produce a minimum of seven to nine pregnancies that would all need to result in normal footed calves or inspected fetus to insure a minimum 97 percent probability she was not a carrier. Wayne Hay was labeled "TM," tested a non-carrier of the mule foot gene, and that put BLACKSTAR in the clear to come to Select Sires.

7HO1897 To-Mar BLACKSTAR

BLACKSTAR was a magnificent black, silky hided bull that went on to score Excellent (93) and became the No. 1 TPI proven sire in the breed as a first-crop proven sire and again as a 99 percent reliability sire. BLACKSTAR turned out to be a global giant,

impacting sire and dam pedigrees around the world. BLACKSTAR was famous for siring silky, black dairy cows with great feet and legs and udders with solid production. He turned out to be a health trait sire before health traits were summarized; he sired high Productive Life (PL), low Somatic Cell Score (SCS) and high Daughter Pregnancy Rate (DPR), all traits for longer lasting cows. Today, BLACKSTAR ranks as the No. 8 sire for genes

BLACKSTAR is joined by ELEVATION, BELL, MARK, MANDINGO, and BERETTA as sires having memorials at Select Sires.

in common in the breed. One of BLACKSTAR's greatest impact sons would have to be 7HO3948 MJR Blackstar EMORY-ET (EX-97-GM), the sire of 7HO5708 Fustead BLITZ-ET (EX-95-GM) both great impact sires in their own right." –Charlie Will

7HO3948 MJR Blackstar EMORY-ET (EX-97-GM)

7HO3948 MJR Blackstar EMORY-ET (EX-97-GM)

"I stopped at Richters Dairy in Southern Illinois to see a high-index 7HO1118 Arlinda ROTATE (EX-92-GM) daughter that showed up on the elite cow list. When the breeder and I went to the cow lot to see MJR Rotate Elsie (VG-88), we passed a pen of bulls. Mike mentioned "that speckled bull is a BLACKSTAR son of Elsie," he was eating at the bunk and was a very impressive individual. We went on to the cow lot to see Elsie. Wow, she was a big, wide, powerful cow with a fantastic udder. She would be an easy Excellent in most herds, maybe even (91) or (92) scored at the right time. The limiting factor was the score of her dam, she was a 78-point 7HO702 Huberview MILESTONE daughter, but the third dam was a Very Good ELEVATION daughter. Mike got very limited interest from other studs due to the score of the dam. Then we saw two really nice milking daughters of Elsie by a very bad bull, Trifecta, so I figured if this cow can make really good daughters of a bad bull, I wonder how good this BLACKSTAR son could turn out to be. When we went back past the bull-

7HO3948 MJR BLACKSTAR Emory-ET (EX-97-GM)

pen, EMORY was still eating. I made Mike a low cash price offer and he said it's better than a herd bull price, he's yours. EMORY went on to sire big, strong cows with an amazing will to milk, from super udders and outstanding feet and legs. That good-looking, young bull calf at the farm went on to classify Excellent (97) points, the highest possible score an animal can achieve. EMORY's greatest impact son, 7HO5708 Fustead Emory BLITZ-ET (EX-95-GM), continues his legacy." –Charlie Will

7HO3707 Paradise-R Cleitus MATHIE (EX-96-GM)

"MATHIE was sired by Bis-May Tradition Cleitus, the highest TPI sire at the time, best known as an extreme production bull. Cleitus turned out to be a great match on Bell Sears, an Excellent big-time production 7HO543 Carlin-M Ivanhoe BELL daughter. She was backed by a great type pedigree, the second dam was an (EX-92) Sexation daughter and the third dam was an

7H3707 Paradise-R Cleitus MATHIE used a combination of type and milk production improvement to join the million unit club at Select Sires.

(EX-91) Milu daughter. MATHIE was very popular as a first-crop proven sire, but his real claim to fame was how his daughters developed in second, third, fourth, fifth lactation

7HO3707 Paradise R Cleitus MATHIE

cows and beyond. MATHIE quickly became a favorite of Select Sires SMS evaluators, salesmen and customers, which resulted in MATHIE going on to be one of Select Sires' only three bulls to sell over 1.5 million units of semen over his lifetime. When we sell that amount of semen, a bull has to have two things: He has to be able to produce a lot of semen over his lifetime and he has to be in great semen demand; MATHIE did both of those things well. MATHIE went on to be one of the longest lived bulls ever at Select Sires, and classified an impressive Excellent (96) at 15 years, six-months-of-age.

Like his daughters, MATHIE got better with age and became a household name for siring longer-lasting, highly productive cows. He excelled in fitness traits before they became fashionable." –Charlie Will

7HO2236 Emprise Bell ELTON*CV (EX-95)

7HO2236 Emprise Bell ELTON

"When this breeder-proven bull came out with a high proof on his first summary I called the breeder and owner, David Jennissen in Minnesota, and mentioned Select Sires had some interest in the bull. I would like to come up and see the daughters of the bull. I set up an appointment and flew to Minneapolis the next week, rented a car and drove to the farm in Sauk Centre. When I arrived, I asked Dave where most of the milking daughters were located. He looked at me puzzled and said, "I thought you knew where they were." This was a really good sign to me that this bull was honestly and randomly sampled. I had the BEAD list from USDA and we proceeded to the local DHIA center to look up herd codes on the BEAD list, then write down the names and addresses and phone numbers of owners of the ELTON daughters, and finally we set off on our trip to see as many milking daughters as we could. At most herds, we had to tell the owner what the ear tag and barn name of the cow that we were looking to see, truly a good sign of a random sampled sire. We went to Dave's barn to see ELTON's dam, GLENDELL Effie, she was scored Good Plus (83) and only Good in the mammary. She was a typical GLENDELL daughter, big and strong, milked like crazy, but had plenty of udder. When we went to see the bull, wow, he was an impressive individual. I really wanted this bull in our barn at Select Sires. The ELTON daughters were very uniform in type, they were moderate in stature and had great feet and legs and well attached, silky udders, not fancy, but gave a lot of milk.

"We negotiated a lease contract for ELTON and he came to Select Sires. ELTON was a very high-ranking bull as a first-crop sire but when he got his second-crop daughters he turned out to be even better than his first-crop daughter data had indicated. EL-TON went on to follow in BELL's footsteps to be one of the breed's greatest impact sires for production from great type cows. ELTON went on to classify an impressive Excellent (95) at 11 years- of- age. ELTON sired the greatest type sire of all-time, 7HO5157 Regancrest Elton DURHAM-ET*CV (EX-90-GM) and the maternal grandsire of the greatest commercial producers' sire of all-time, 7HO6417 O-Bee MANfred Justice-ET (EX-94-GM)." –Charlie Will

7HO4213 Robthom INTEGRITY-ET (EX-96-GM)

"This Gold Medal sire was a premier bull for Select during the 1990s. An impressive individual, he mirrored what his daughters looked like, cows with a tall, uphill run, great modern length of neck and body, clean boned with great rear udders. This BLACK-STAR son from the great Robthom Ivory Mark, also Excellent (94), left the legacy as a million unit selling sire as well.

7HO4213 Robthom INTEGRITY was one of a select group with over 1.4 million units of sales. L-R: Mark Eades, Brian Spires, Rick Barker, Greg Thomas, Jeremy Roberts and Pat Jones.

7HO4213 Robthom INTEGRITY

7HO4213 Robthom INTEGRITY is joined by Dale Pennington, Blaine Crosser, Clif Marshall, and Dave Thorbahn in his recognition of selling 1 million units.

INTEGRITY offered high udder composite, show ring style and high milk for the time, all the same attributes delivered from the breeding establishment: Robthom Holsteins! INTEGRITY just set the path around the world as one of the best 'BLACKSTAR x MARK' crosses." -Scott Culbertson

7HO5157 Regancrest Elton DURHAM-ET *CV (EX-90-GM)

7HO5157 Regancrest Elton DURHAM

"The good Lord was shining on Select the day DURHAM left Iowa to come to Select Sires. There were four ELTON sons of the great Excellent (95) show cow, Snow-N Denises Dellia (EX-95-2E-EX-MS-GMD-DOM), by MARK, better known as Della.

Alta had first choice, Japan had second choice and Select had third choice. Good thing genomics had not yet been invented, Select may have not ended up with the greatest type sire of all time. DURHAM got the best of his great parents, the balance of his sire ELTON, the good fitness traits of calving ease (CE), low SCS and good DPR and super feet and legs. The stature and style of Della's famous sire MARK, and a second shot of balance from his Excellent (93) BELL grandam.

"DURHAM started like a tall, gangly young teenager. He classified Good Plus (83) on his first score, but got better with age, just like his daughters do and he classified Excellent at 7-years 6-months-of-age.

"DURHAM became one of the first five-time consecutive Premier Sire winners at World Dairy Expo's National Holstein Show. Still today, DURHAM is the standard by which all other would-be great type sires are compared. What was truly different than all the Premier Sires at Expo that came before him, DURHAM actually sired the traits that commercial dairymen were looking for, low SCS, good calving ease, good daughter fertility and cows that lasted and improved with age." –Charlie Will

7HO5157 Regancrest Elton DURHAM

7HO6417 O-Bee MANfred Justice-ET (EX-94-GM)

"This Manfred son is from one of ELTON's most impressive daughters, Meier-Meadows El Jezebel (EX-92-EX-MS-GMD-DOM). She was a ton cow, big and strong and wide, milked from strength and managed very well in the Obert's free stall environment. Lady Luck was truly on Select Sires' side for

7HO6417 Obee Manfred Justice (OMAN)

O MAN to become a 7H sire. There were three bulls in a flush with Genex having first choice. They made their choice which left two bulls, one very impressive calf and another just average. It came down to Obert's making a decision whether to take a high cash offer from Japan or take Select Sires' lease offer in hopes it would pay off in the long run. They decided to gamble on the long term and O MAN came to Select Sires and re-wrote the history books."

Gaylon and Jeannie Obert stand with one of their sires, 7HO6417 O-Bee Manfred Justice (O MAN)

"It turned out O MAN's dam, Jezebel, carried both CV and BL recessive genes, but O MAN dodged the bullet and did not inherit either recessive gene, only the good genes of his great cow family.

"O MAN set a record for the number of times a bull held the No. 1 spot on Holsteins' TPI list, even after he reached 99 percent reliability. O MAN was also the first bull to be the No. 1 ranked sire in 10 countries, based on milking daughter data within their perspective countries. O MAN's success rate for top proven sons and grandsons is unheralded and his impact in the breed around the world will be hard to match for generations to come. O MAN has probably made commercial breeders milking his daughters more money than any bull in history." –Charlie Will

7HO5375 Mara-Thon BW MARSHALL-ET (VG-86-GM)

7HO5375 Mara-Thon BW MARSHALL

"BW MARSHALL was the result of the magic combination of a big-time production sire, Bellwood, on a great type cow, Morgan-Valley Elton Mara (VG-87-GMD-DOM). Elton Mara was one of the highest type index cows in the breed at the time, with over +3.00 PTAT, +3.00 UDC and +3.00 FLC. Elton

Mara was never classified in her prime; she was scored Very Good (87) but could have easily been Excellent (92) with an Excellent mammary if she were classified early in her third lactation. Elton Mara was a big, strong cow with a fantastic udder and feet and legs. The third dam was a MELVIN daughter and that size and width of rump came through in Mara. BW MARSHALL dodged the BL recessive bullet and went on to be a very popular sire of great-framed cows with an exceptional will to milk. BW MARSHALL made an impact in the breed through his popular sons like 7HO7536 COLDSPRINGs Kenyon 9118-ET (EX-92), 7HO7838 GLEN-Valley BW Captain-ET (EX-94), 7HO7156 Honeycrest ELEGANT-ET (GM), 7HO8444 Chan-Lee Marshal GRAYBIL-ET and 7HO7466 Robthom MOSCOW-ET (EX-94-GM)." –Charlie Will

7HO5708 Fustead Emory BLITZ-ET (EX-95-GM)

"BLITZ is a double BLACK-STAR grandson. He is sired by EMORY and his grandam is one of the very early Excellent BLACKSTAR daughters. She in turn is out of an Excellent (90) MARK and then a BELL. BLITZ continues to hold the lifetime semen sales record at Select Sires with more than 1.52 million units sold.

7HO5708 Fustead Emory BLITZ

"BLITZ most closely follows his sire EMORY's breeding pattern, big, strong, powerful cows with great udders, exceptional feet and legs and an amazing will to milk. BLITZ was a favorite of SMS evaluators as his conformation traits could quickly improve a frail or low-producing cow family in one generation of breeding. BLITZ has made a big impact around the world, siring high scoring cows with record-breaking milk production. BLITZ was a very impressive individual classifying Excellent (95) at 12- years and 6 months-of-age. Fustead Farms, owned by Brian and Wendy Fust is a small family farm in northern

Charlie Will stands with Brian and Wendy Fust, the breeders of Fustead Emory BLITZ, under the watchful eye of the Select Sires million unit producer.

Wisconsin that has made a big impact at Select Sires. The Fusts bred BLITZ and one of Blitz's most popular grandsons, 7HO9420 Fustead Goldwyn GUTHRIE-ET, also Excellent (94) points, whose dam is an Excellent BLITZ daughter." –Charlie Will

7HO6782 Ocean-View ZENITH-TW-ET (GM)

7HO6782 Oceanview ZENITH

"ZENITH was an early DURHAM son from the great Ocean-View Mandel Zandra (EX-95-2E-EX-MS-GMD-DOM) with a legacy of great cows in his pedigree and was developed to be the next great type bull of the breed. But his own legacy was made in his reputation as a trouble-free, modern-made, health trait specialist. ZENITH was a breed-leading low SCS bull with strong PL, DPR and silky udders. His daughters weren't the show cows Select was looking for, but customer satisfaction ranked strong and commercial dairymen gobbled him up for longevity purposes." –Scott Culbertson

7HO6025 De-Matt Rudolph TEAMSTER-ET (GM)

7HO6025 De-Matt Rudolph TEAMSTER

"TEAMSTER had an interesting path at Select Sires. His cross of Rudolph x Mascot meant one thing: we were not expecting a great foot angle! When TEAMSTER debuted on the top 100 TPI list, the decision was made to activate the bull. He delivered huge milk, low SCS, strong PL traits with real dairy cows and wide rear udders, but the daughters did have spongy pasterns.

After a few runs and great semen bank, Select made the decision to export the bull for a large amount of money. Lo and behold, when his second crop arrived, his overall proof went up 100 TPI points, and breeders liked the daughters. They had great udder quality, were tall cows and they flat out milked! It appeared the foot angle didn't bother anyone too much. He still impacted our bloodlines and now people like to see him in a pedigree." -Scott Culbertson

7HO8175 Windy-Knoll-View PRONTO-ET (EX-95)

"PRONTO was privately sampled by his breeder, the Burdette Family of Pennsylvania, Hank VanExel and JLG enterprises both of California. When PRONTO came out with a daughter data proof he ranked near the top of the TPI list and had a great type pedigree that breeders dream about. PRONTO

7HO8175 Windy Knoll View PRONTO

was sired by Outside, a high ranking LPI and highly respected Canadian proven sire. PRONTO's dam was an Excellent (95) successful show cow, Windy-Knoll-View Rudolph Promis, and the next dam was also a successful Excellent (94) point cow. Starting out with a very high proof and sampled across the U.S. with many more daughters to come, this great-pedigreed sire was an outcross to most of Select Sires' popular sire lines, making PRONTO a must have for Select Sires.

"The competition was keen for the bull, but after much negotiation the owners chose to send PRONTO to Select Sires. PRONTO was housed at JLG enterprises, a custom collection facility in California that Select had worked with for many years and we all agreed he would stay at JLG for housing and collection.

"PRONTO was a very popular bull in Select Sires' program and when his second-crop daughters started to freshen they were every bit as good as his original first-crop daughters. He sired great dairy strength, width of chest, exceptional feet and legs, and well-attached udders and the daughters were solid milk and components producers. PRONTO went on to score Excellent (95) as did his full sister, Outside Pledge and maternal sister

Durham Pammy. Pronto's highest TPI ranking proven son also resides at Select Sires. 7HO10643 MR BC Dana Pronto DWAYNE (EX-91), who recently classified Excellent 91." –Charlie Will

7HO7466 Robthom MOSCOW-ET (EX-94-GM)

"MOSCOW was another great graduate from Robthom Holsteins! An early B W MARSHALL son from an Excellent (92) INTEGRITY daughter brought storied success from the farm to Select Sires. Different than INTEGRITY daughters, MOSCOW daughters were durable, tough cows, with plain rumps, but they had silky udders and he was bred to be a leading low SCS bull. The best trait of MOSCOW was great conception. He just settled everything and was popular with all technicians. A great milk sire for the times with good SCR made him popular enough to be another million unit selling sire from Robthom!" –Scott Culbertson

7HO7466 Robthom MOSCOW

7HO6758 Regancrest-MR Drhm SAM-ET (GM)

"MR SAM delivered the time-tested cross of "DURHAM x EMORY." A popular Super Sampler™, his dam was a typical EMORY with a strong front end and a big cage. His pedigree included an Excellent (91) Prelude grandam and she brought all the components to the pedigree. The MR SAM's were not flashy like the DURHAM's, or as tall, but the hard loins, width of chest and high, wide rear udders put smiles on many customers who had them. Now with over 70,000 daughters in his proof solidifying his traits, he is a strong cheese market

7HO6758 Regancrest MR Durham SAM (MR SAM)

bull due to his components. He sired consistent type pattern and great leg mobility and his world-wide popularity was strong everywhere he was used." –Scott Culbertson

7HO8165 England-Ammon MILLION-ET (EX-92-GM)

"MILLION was appropriately named as a calf, as he went on to sell over 1 million units of semen in his lifetime. MILLION quickly gained popularity as being one of the most fertile semen bulls in the breed. He was used to settle some of the most difficult breeding cows and heifers, and both breeders and A.I. technicians alike used MILLION as the go to

7HO8165 England-Ammon MILLION

bull to get cows pregnant. High semen fertility, low calving ease score and cows that milk well from dairy strength along with great feet and legs that can handle concrete were the main reasons that contributed to MILLION reaching the million unit sales milestone. This Outside son was from a BW MARSHALL dam and a Rudolph grandam that was a maternal sister to none other than DURHAM. MILLION's own width and depth and exceptional feet and legs contributed to his Excellent (92) final score." -Charlie Will

7HO7615 Solid-Gold COLBY-ET (EX-93-GM)

7HO7615 Solid Gold COLBY

"An Outside son from a Rudolph dam and Conquest grandam made COLBY a unique outcross from the traditional and popular Select Sires bloodlines. This also made COLBY an easy bull to use to control inbreeding.

"COLBY was popular based on his first crop daughter data proof as a high component, outstanding type conformation sire with high DPR and PL traits. As his second-crop daughters began to freshen he really caught the eye of the SMS evaluators, as his daughters were some of the most eye-appealing young cows in the herds they evaluated. As time went on and COLBY daughters calved back in their second and third lactations, they kept getting better with age for type and production and he became famous for high daughter fertility resulting in continued popularity growth. Even today his milk proof is higher than his first-crop proof, evidence his daughters gained in lifetime production each and every lactation. COLBY improved with age rising to the score of Excellent (93) points at 9-years and 5-months-of-age.

"Today it is very desirable to have COLBY in a pedigree, he is well respected as a sire of long-lasting, beautiful cows." -Charlie Will

7HO7536 COLDSPRINGs Kenyon 9118-ET (EX-92)

7HO7536 COLDSPRINGs Kenyon

"Bred by Marlin Hoff and acquired by Ron Long, the mating of BW MARSHALL to 9HO1729 Brabant Star PATRON-ET (EX-92-GM) daughters was a very popular and successful mating. COLDSPRING's dam and grandam were Excellent (90) and Excellent (94) and both carried Excellent mammary systems. The unique quality both his dam and grandam transmitted to COLDSPRING was their wide frames and square rumps. You can see these qualities in the COLDSPRING daughters. During COLDSPRING's first crop period, he had to compete with several paternal brothers that resulted from the same combination of BW MARSHALL x PATRON. His second-crop proof allowed COLDSPRING to separate from his paternal brothers and become recognized as one of BW MARSHALL's best sons. COLDSPRING has become a tremendous customer satisfaction sire. He sires the "right size" cow for today's commercial dairy operations. The COLDSPRING daughters also possess quality mammary systems and trouble-free feet and legs. His outstanding fertility and calving ease have contributed to COLDSPRING becoming regarded as one of BW MARSHALL's best all-around sons." -Rick VerBeek

7HO7838 GLEN-Valley BW Captain-ET (EX-94)

"There were many more popular BW MARSHALL sons than GLEN based on first-crop daughter proof information, but when the dust settled with thousands of second-crop daughters and many now in second and third lactations, GLEN has risen near the top as one of the greatest BW MARSHALL sons. One of the things that limited Glen's popularity as a first-crop sire was the fact his dam was a 7HO4637 Ladys-Manor WINCHESTER-ET (EX-95-GM) daughter. WINCHESTER was famous as a great production sire, but his daughters' udders did not wear well over time. GLEN's dam was the most impressive WINCHESTER daughter I ever saw. She went Very Good 89-points as a two-year-old and later went on to score Excellent (93) points. The power of this great

7HO7838 GLEN Valley BW Captain

cow family traces back to the Excellent (92) Blackstar Classy great grandam, no matter what sire you used on her she transmitted great type. GLEN was a tall, fancy and stylish bull scoring Excellent (94) at less than five-years-of-age.

"GLEN's popularity quickly grew when his second-crop daughters began to freshen. Every herd milking his daughters loved them and wanted more just like them. The SMS and sales teams became true believers in GLEN as a great sire and soon forgave the fact that his dam was a WINCHESTER daughter. GLEN is highly respected today as a bull that will sire tall, stylish cows with amazing udders, high components and easy calving. His daughters tend to get better with age, develop into great mature cows and become good brood cows with which to build a strong cow family." –Charlie Will

Daughter group of 7HO7838 GLEN

7HO7872 KHW Kite ADVENT-RED-ET (EX-94)

7HO7872 KHW Kite ADVENT-RED

"ADVENT-RED also had an interesting path to Select Sires. He was sired by a competitor's young sire at the time. We had never sampled a bull that way before. He was a rough looking calf, kind of sickly. A Kite son from a phenomenal DURHAM two-year-old, then an Excellent (93) Prelude and a legacy of high-scoring cows marked his pedigree. When he ended up failing health tests to come to headquarters, the decision was made to release him and send him to Glaz-Way Enterprises, LLC for sampling. About the time of his release, Select was really short on Red Holsteins to sample, so the decision was made to bring him back to headquarters as a Super Sampler. When the calves hit the ground and started showing at World Dairy Expo, the excitement grew. By the time his daughters started to calve, everyone worldwide knew of his greatness!

7HO7872 KHW Kite ADVENT-RED

His daughters dominated the show ring like no other red bull had done. Modern made with DURHAM-like udders, they matured so greatly. A four-time Premier Red & White sire at World Dairy Expo marked his legacy. He is still used today to make the special one!"-Scott Culbertson

7HO7004 Erbacres DAMION (EX-96)

"DAMION was a controversial bull for Select the day he arrived. Believed to be the only brother x sister cross ever sampled in A.I., DAMION delivered as promised in the best example of line-breeding. His family was great from his Very Good (89) 9HO1833 Marcrest ENCORE (EX-96-GM) dam and then the immortal Snow-N

7HO7004 Erbacres DAMION

Denises Dellia (EX-95-2E-EX-MS-GMD-DOM) on both sides of his pedigree! DAMION was the No. 1 bull sampled for Type in his sampling year. And when he re-

7HO7004 Erbacres DAMION

ceived his first sire summary, he was again the No. 1 Type bull of the breed! DAMION's daughters are different than DURHAM's, not the flash and length of body, but big rib cages, hard loins and phenomenal udders. As they continued to calve and mature, everyone liked them better. When Damion received his full second-crop sire summary, he again was the No.1 bull for Type at 99 percent Reliability. It was a great finish for a well-bred bull who stamped his niche from beginning to end!" -Scott Culbertson

7HO8081 Ensenada Taboo PLANET-ET (EX-90-GM)

7HO8081 Ensenada Taboo PLANET

"PLANET was born in the herd of David and Josh Bishop of Doylestown, Pa. This 75-cow tie-stall herd is a family-run operation, whose main focus at the time PLANET was created was breeding a nice herd of cows that would pay the bills with the milk they produced. Since that time, merchandising genetics from their breeding program has become another aspect of their breeding program due to the success of the Patty family. The idea behind the mating that produced PLANET was to create an outcross sire that would produce profitable cattle for commercial dairymen. It also was about working with Amel Patty, a young cow that had a great mammary system and an incredible will to milk. PLANET is a bull that at the beginning of his career was considered an outcross sire. Due to his ability to consistently transmit his extreme qualities to his sons and daughters, when his career is finished he can no longer be considered an outcross. To me, the PLANET daughters are mirror images of Amel Patty. PLANET is one of the best pure production sires the breed has ever seen. He is also one of the best "profit" sires the breed has seen. His pattern of siring moderate frames, outstanding mammary systems and huge production has been in demand around the world. His impact is just beginning to be revealed as his sons and grandsons carry on the PLANET legacy." -Rick VerBeek

The Bishop family of Ensenada Holsteins with a picture of the August 2012 Holstein directory featuring 7HO8081 Ensenada Taboo PLANET.

7HO8221 Golden-Oaks ST ALEXANDER-ET (EX-94)

"ALEXANDER debuted as one of the early, high-ranking proven Stormatic sons in the U.S. He offered a little different pedigree for breeders to choose from. ALEXANDER's high index dam sold for more than $52,000 at public auction and her dam, Aerostar Allie, was at one time, the No. 1 TPI cow in the breed. ALEXANDER became well known for siring black, silky hided, moderate-statured cows with exceptional feet and legs and snugly attached udders. ALEXANDER has shown that he can sire the show-winning kind as well with several class winners at World Dairy Expo. You can usually spot the ALEXANDER daughters in a show ring. Look for the silky, nearly all black animal and it will likely be an ALEXANDER daughter. ALEXANDER himself is impressive - tall, dairy and stylish with that silky black hide that gets him to his Excellent (94) final score." -Charlie Will

7HO8221 Golden Oaks ST ALEXANDER

7HO8190 Gen-Mark Stmatic SANCHEZ (EX-94)

7HO8190 GenMark Stmatic SANCHEZ

Daughter of 7HO8190 SANCHEZ, Valleyville Rae Lynn

"Markland Holsteins and Genetic Co., Macedon, N.Y. provided Select Sires with SANCHEZ. The mating behind SANCHEZ might not have started out as "conventional" at the time, but it has produced some amazing results. The idea was to use a high type sire, Stormatic, on a high production and high type maternal family (even though the sires in the pedigree might not have suggested high type). The goal was to produce a balanced production and type sire that could also be a high TPI sire. While some "pedigree experts" might have doubted SANCHEZ's ability to sire high scoring, even All-American type, seeing is believing. The power and type of the Hillary family combined with Stormatic produced one of the breed's dominant type sires of his era. SANCHEZ is one of the breed's highest second crop type sires of all time. He will be regarded as an extreme frame sire that improves width and depth like few bulls before him. One of the nice things about SANCHEZ is that while he competes with the best for type, the SANCHEZ daughters also know how to milk." –Rick VerBeek

7HO8747 End-Road O-Man BRONCO-ET (EX-93-GM)

"BRONCO was one of those good looking bulls you would see at our Darby Creek sire in waiting barns that you hoped would make it as a proven bull because he was so impressive to look at and he garnished an impressive Excellent (93) score as a young bull. Fortunately, BRONCO graduated as a high-rank-

7HO8747 End Road O-Man BRONCO

ing proven sire and gained popularity quickly as a high production sire with exceptional fitness traits, solid type conformation traits and a reputation as one of the breed's best calving ease sires. Unfortunately, BRONCO died of a twisted intestine before his second crop daughters began to freshen and his real impact was revealed. After seeing hundreds of milking second-crop daughters, it is evident BRONCO was going to be a great bull and possibly O MAN's greatest son. Today, BRONCO ranks in the top dozen TPI bulls on Holstein's 97 percent or higher Reliability list. BRONCO is sought after in any pedigree and he will likely have many top proven sons and grandsons to carry on his legacy for generations to come." –Charlie Will

7HO8559 Macomber O-Man BOGART

"It's all in the family in more ways than one. One of the breeders of O MAN is Gaylon Obert in northern Illinois; the breeder of BOGART is his brother-in-law and neighbor, David Macomber. Great breeders think alike. David had so much confidence in his brother-in-law's bull, O MAN, that he bred his best cow to him, which resulted in a bull that went on to be one of the breed's best time-tested sires. BOGART writes a unique maternal side being from an Excellent (90) 7HO5592 Wil-Hart E LOUIE-ET (EX-93-GM) and then an Excellent (90) 7HO4638

7HO8559 Macomber O-Man BOGART

Ricecrest Tesk TER-RY (GP-82-GM) grandam and a Very Good (88) ELTON great grandam. BO-GART's second-crop daughters confirmed his consistent breeding pattern, tall strong daughters with exceptional feet and legs, solid udder improver and outstanding calving ease, all traits that do well in all herd environments. BOGA-

7HO8559 Macomber O-Man BOGART

RT's extremely high components made him a perfect fit for breeders in a cheese producing milk market. BOGART also ranks in the breed's Top 20 TPI 97 percent Reliability list for time-tested sires." –Charlie Will

7HO8856 Ri-Val-Re 2338 NIAGRA-ET (GM)

"NIAGRA graduated as one of the breed's top-ranked proven sires as a real outcross opportunity. He was an early Boliver son from an Excellent (91) Jesther daughter. Jesther was a high-ranking proven bull from France with a limited amount of semen coming to the U.S. NIAGRA dodged the recessive bullet for Complex Vertebral

7HO8856 Ri-Val-Re 2338 NIAGRA

Malformation (CV), with two crosses back to ELTON, his maternal grandsire Jesther was CV positive and NIAGRA's TERRY dam was CV positive, which came from her Excellent ELTON dam who was also a CV carrier. Adding a touch of type was a MELVIN fifth dam.

"NIAGRA died before his second-crop daughters began to freshen, limiting what was to most certainly be one of the breed's great and unique sires. NIAGRA is still one of the breed's best milk sires with exceptional udders and his easy calving made him a natural sire to use in any heifer A.I. program. NIAGRA came along at the right point in time to use as an ideal mating on all the Shottle blood in the breed. NIAGRA is much in demand to have in a pedigree. He added lots of milk and fine udders."-Charlie Will

7HO8477 Willow-Marsh-CC GABOR-ET (EX-94-GM)

"GABOR was the result of a contract mating working with Chuck Curtis and J.R. Arnold, Ballston Spa, N.Y. and Johcar Convicer Gama-ET when she was a Very Good (86) two-year- old. The flush resulted in six bulls and two females. The two females are now scored Excellent (90) and Very Good

7HO8477 Willow-Marsh-CC GABOR

(87). Three of the bulls were sampled; GABOR, one by ABS and one by Alta. Select had the first choice domestic bull from this flush. Japan had the first choice overall, but was unable to purchase a bull due to health restrictions at the time (BSE, if I remember correctly). GABOR was selected prior to the advent of genomics, sometimes it pays to be lucky. He is a high customer-satisfaction sire. His daughters have tremendously wide frames. He might be one of the best width bulls in the breed today, very wide front and rear-ended cattle. Their ability to produce milk (GABOR has been a top 10- milk bull in the U.S.) and have very pleasing type is a great combination. When you then factor in his outstanding fitness traits it makes it easy to see why so many customers appreciate him. GABOR has been an extremely popular bull for Select Sires. He was a top-4 selling bull for us four out of the last five years going into 2013. His lifetime sales total was just shy of 1 million units and popular countries for Gabor were the U.S., Canada, Italy, Spain, Japan and France."-Rick VerBeek

7HO9222 Lincoln-Hill SHOT Laser-ET (EX-92)

7HO9222 Lincoln Hill SHOT Laser

"SHOT was a resulting mating from working with Leonard Austin in Eagle Bridge, N.Y. Sometimes timing is everything in sire acquisition; the mating that produced SHOT was all about timing! Picston Shottle had just burst onto the scene with a huge proof increase a few months after semen had started to be marketed here in the U.S. At the same time, Lincoln-Hill Ito Nibbles (VG-88-GMD-DOM) was fresh and one of the early second-crop daughters of Barbee-M Juror Ito (EX-90-GM). The strengths and weaknesses of Shottle and Ito Nibbles complemented each other very well, so Lenny and I agreed to locate some Shottle semen and flush Nibbles for a Select Sires contract. SHOT is the result of that mating. SHOT's story continues to unfold as the 50th anniversary book goes to print. However one thing is apparent, SHOT is the most prolific semen producer in Select Sires history. In 2012, SHOT became the first bull in Select Sires history to surpass 300,000 units sold in one year. In just a little over three years as an active sire, SHOT's lifetime semen sales had already exceed 750,000 units sold. He has become one of the youngest "millionaire" sires in the breed. SHOT's "no-holes" proof, combined with outstanding semen production resulted in a bull that is popular around the world."-Rick VerBeek

7HO10506 Maple-Downs-I G W ATWOOD-ET (EX-90)

"G W ATWOOD is the most significant type-improving sire in the breed since DURHAM and Goldwyn. Like his sire and maternal grandsire, G W ATWOOD will most certainly become Premier Sire at World Dairy Expo many times over the next decade. He is the No. 1 PTAT sire in the breed, proven or genomic, and he is 99 percent Reliable for Type, an indication he will be near the top of the Type list for many years to come. G W ATWOOD was bred for type with his great sire stack and his extraordinary Durham Atlee cow family. Yet, it took genomics to identify G W ATWOOD as likely the best type bull of five full brothers born in a herd in Canada. The first four choices were made by various A.I. studs, leaving the ugly duckling G W ATWOOD still on the farm. He was then syndicated by a group including Glaz-Way Enterprises, LLC of California. Some semen had been collected and marketed and then G W

7HO10506 Maple-Downs-I GW ATWOOD

ATWOOD's genomic proof came out in early 2009, and he was the No. 1 Type bull in the breed, and by a large margin. Select aggressively negotiated for rights to lease the bull, and after several months of back and forth negotiations, Select was awarded the contract to market the bull. "As confidence in genomics grew, so did the demand for this high genomic type sire. Daughters began to freshen in early 2012 and the excitement began to build as they were every bit as good for type as his genomic data predicted. G W ATWOOD received his first official type proof in August of 2012 and it confirmed he was the best in the breed. Today his daughters dominate the heifer and cow classes at the major shows and he is gaining many high, new Excellent daughters scored every day. G W ATWOOD, the new global household name around the world for extraordinary type." –Charlie Will

7JE177 Highland Magic DUNCAN

7JE177 Highland Magic DUNCAN

Daughter of 7JE177 DUNCAN, Silverstream Duncan Peg

"Born Sept 1, 1980, this bull was a breed-changer. So much in fact, I remember having non-Jersey breeders calling me and asking questions about the Jersey bull that had daughters that even Holstein breeders would want. DUNCAN was born in Maine, but sampled by Jerseyland Sires in California. Rodger Hoyt and Scott Johnson evaluated the milking daughters in the spring of 1985 and quickly knew he was a bull Select Sires had to have in their program. DUNCAN quickly became a breed leader, ranking No.1 in the breed from July 1986 to January 1988. His daughters excelled in production with dairy frames of width and depth, and udders not found in the breed up until his time. He was the perfect cross on SOONER bloodlines, so that combination became the norm of every Jersey breeder. DUNCAN ended his A.I. career much too early, as he tested positive for Johnes Disease in mid-1987. At that time, Select Sires taught the industry how to handle a bull with Johnes by conducting a semen test on every ejaculation to assure users that Johnes was not transmitted in his semen. In July 1988, he succumbed to this fatal disease. DUNCAN went on to be a huge success as a sire of proven sons (7JE207 Rebob Duncan HERMITAGE-ET being his first), maternal grandsire of many highly proven sons and was premier sire of the 1990 and 1991 All American Jersey show."- Jeff Ziegler

7JE159 Soldierboy Boomer SOONER of CJ

"Born February 25, 1983, this Briarcliffs Soldier Boy son from a Generator HL Earl dam was the pure production bull that put the breed on the new plain of high volumes of milk production never seen before. Acquired from Ellis Woods of Gage, Okla., John Hecker had the sharp eye and quick trigger to outpace others that later wanted this bull, already slated to head to Plain City, Ohio. SOONER quickly proved to be the No. 1 milk bull of the breed and had 70-and 80-pound two year-olds that breeder's weren't accustomed to. I remember his first two-year-olds I saw were at Buttercrest Jerseys in Ohio, and they were ultra-dairy, silky uddered cows that spent most of their time at the feed bunk. Not of show type, but udder quality that allowed large volumes of milk to come from udders that were nothing but tissue once milked out. Springing SOONERS could give concern as they looked like heifers that could blow their udder, but it was just their early will to milk. In fact, many breeders started to milk their SOONER daughters even prior to calving. SOONER was a huge maternal success, but without question his lasting mark was left by his son 7JE254 Mason Boomer Sooner BERRETTA." - Jeff Ziegler

7JE254 Mason Boomer Sooner BERRETTA

"BERRETTA was born March 18, 1989. No bull in Jersey history, past or present, has led the breed for total index as BERRETTA did for 13 consecutive sire summaries! This early SOONER son out of an Excellent (91) Early Settler daughter was the talk of the 1989 National Jersey Convention in Idaho after visiting the Bill Mason herd. I remember meeting Bill Mason while speaking at a series of Cache Valley meetings in 1988. Bill gave me a test sheet on this Early Settler cow that did nothing but milk and milk in some tough Idaho conditions that included no barn or shade in sight for the cows 365 days a year. Bill Mason had a passion for Jerseys like few others, and led the cheese yield charge, particularly in breeding for protein. He called me when BERRETTA was born and made my decision an easy

7JE254 Mason Boomer Sooner BERETTA

one to bring this bull to the Select Sires program. Little did I know, this bull would launch the breed into a profit-oriented situation that created breed growth that still is in mode today. BERRETTA could make a show cow, a great commercial cow, a great brood cow and do it on a variety of bloodlines. More than 20 sons of BERRETTA were

sampled by Select Sires alone as it was very difficult to find another sire that even compared in value. BERRETTA was so dominant; he also became the original bull for Holstein breeders beginning an organized crossbreeding program of Jersey semen on the Holstein heifers. He is the only Jersey sire to earn a headstone still proudly displayed at Select Sires headquarters today." –Jeff Ziegler

Jeff Ziegler presents two bull rings to Bill Mason, breeder of Mason Boomer Sooner BERRETTA at the dedication ceremony for the BERRETTA memorial.

7JE535 Windy Willow Montana JACE

7JE535 Windy Willow Montana JACE

"JACE was born June 15, 1996. A new bull entered the top ranks in 1998 as a high production sire with quality type named Montana from ABS. After searching some listings, I found a son already born at Windy Willow Farms from a Malcolm daughter out of a DUNCAN that I had seen from a previous visit that really caught my eye. She was an extremely deep ribbed, deep udder cleft cow with a bit more udder, but had incredible production too. This in turn ended up defining what the JACE daughters looked like with great production, deep ribbed frames, exceptional width and a little more udder as two year olds that didn't get worse with successive calvings. JACE became a breed leader for putting capacity in cows with exceptional length, width and depth and adding a dose of stature as well. Used on a smooth show cow, he could and did make blue ribbon winners, used on shallow index cows he could and did make bull dams. Even though several sons were sampled, JACE was still more successful in carrying on his heritage though his milking daughters. JACE also gave our Select Sires veterinarian team a consistent work out with physical ailments all during his career in Plain City. It was not uncommon for a phone call from Dr. Monke to tell me JACE had a new issue (from bloat, to DAs, to stifle concerns) that needed resolved, and always were by our professional team. Again, some of the nicest crossbred cows I saw while traveling the globe were JACE daughters." – Jeff Ziegler

7JE535 Windy Willow Montana JACE

7JE590 Forest Glen Avery ACTION-ET

7JE590 Forest Glen Avery ACTION

"One of the most influential cows to ever sell at the All American Jersey sale was Greenridge FW Chief Althea-ET (E-92%). She was a successful flush cow for her breeder Duane Kuhlman in Washington, her first purchaser, Comfort Hill Jerseys in Vermont and her final owner of Chaney Farms in Kentucky. While Alf, Adonis, and Dunker were her prominent sons, Althea daughters and granddaughters dominated the A.I. world where nearly 10 percent of the U.S. Jersey population could have been traced back paternally or maternally to Althea at one time. It was a BERRETTA granddaughter of Althea that I first saw in the lead stall of the parlor at Forest Glen Farms that I just had to get a son or two from. She had an incredible udder and was as wide-framed as a house. Really wanting to emphasize dairy strength at the time, I convinced Dan Bansen to flush Berretta Addie to Avery and as they say the rest is history. Born June 2, 1999, ACTION went on to become the No. 1 selling Jersey sire in Select Sires history. After a very brief stint as a high ranked sire, he still sires a dairyman's favorite barn cow and still is in huge demand among the show breeder's for putting dairy quality with fabulous udders on the colored shavings. ACTION's sons have been equally successful in selling large volumes

7JE590 Forest Glen Avery ACTION

of semen over their lifetime without being the top-ranked sires of their era. ACTION simply sires the kind of cow dairymen like and want a barn full of: consistent, good uddered, long lived, productive cows." – Jeff Ziegler

164JE1 ISDK Fyn Lemvig

Daughter of 164JE1 LEMVIG, Sunset Canyon Lemvig Ribbon

"Another highly-influential sector of Jersey genetics can be found in the country of Denmark. In the early 1980s, some Danish Jersey semen was used on the U.S. population with very mixed, and mostly unsuccessful results. However, by the late '90s with the onset of Interbull evaluations, Danish sires began to hit these higher-ranking world lists and created a desire in me to try something again. A bull named Lemvig, sired by Duncan Lester, so a 50 percent Danish (Fyn Haug) and 50 percent American-bred bull, was highly-ranked and prompted me to contact the Danish Jersey Breeders Society. After a series of phone calls, I purchased a ticket and headed on my first trip to Denmark. I found herds smaller in size, mostly pasture-based and tie-stall managed in the winter. However, the Lemvig daughters excelled in each of their herds, had great udders, were small framed and looked like a logical choice to follow up on all the BERRETTA influence we had at that point. I flew home and worked with our marketing team to import 2,000 units of Lemvig to test the market. To everyone's surprise, Lemvig was a huge hit as a source of butterfat and a complementary mating such that those 2,000 units quickly disappeared and led to thousands more units of semen to be imported over the next two years. Those short, round Lemvig heifers in the pens gave me some sleepless nights, thinking I may have made a mistake trying these Danish genes again. Thankfully, all turned out fine and Lemvig has gone down in breed history as a success story in influencing every major pocket of Jerseys across the globe. Now with more than 10 countries in his over 28,000-daughter proof, his influence of increased butterfat production from sound, long-lasting udders is unmatched for bulls of his era." – Jeff Ziegler

AYRSHIRE

7AY84 Palmyra Tri-Star BURDETTE-ET

"BURDETTE is one of countless influential Ayrshires deriving from the renowned and well-respected Palmyra Farm in Hagerstown, Md. Their keen ability to breed production animals while balancing type has made Palmyra-bred animals a sought after commodity across the globe and placing more than 80 Ayrshire and Holstein bulls in the A.I. industry, including

Daughter of 7AY84 BURDETTE, Melody Lane Burdette Sally

BURDETTE's sire 9AY75 TRI-STAR. The mating that produced BURDETTE was made by Mary Creek and later contracted by Jeff Ziegler. The dam, Palmyra Reno Bethany-ET, was beloved by Ziegler and as he recalls most notably 'her great rib and dairy strength.' A mating to Palmyra TRI-STAR would double the odds that progeny would also display that favorable body capacity and strength of which BURDETTE daughters are so bestowed with today. On January 12, 2010, 7AY84 Palmyra Tri-Star BURDETTE-ET debuted on the active sire list. While BURDETTE transmits show-winning attributes to his daughters around the globe, he also transmits a change to the small Ayrshire breed. Dairy producers often remark the cows are perfect sized, have extremely desirable feet and legs and they enjoy the cows' fast milking speed and soft udders, simply the kind you like to milk. His daughters have critical commercial function in show type fashion. The fact his daughters continue to be crowd pleasers at competitive shows while still proving they can also milk and make money where it counts is what brings the most pride to the Select Sires federation, and not to mention his breeder Palmyra Farm. Both attributes are achievable. BURDETTE is proof and in doing so is changing the standards of future Ayrshire breeding programs." –Adam Oswalt

BROWN SWISS

*7BS766 Blessing Banker AGENDA ET *TM*

7BS766 Blessing Banker AGENDA

Daughter of 7BS766 AGENDA, Radical Agenda Chelsea

"Directly from one of the breed's most elite cows, Blessing Prophet Ashton *TW "3E91 3E91MS," AGENDA's fat percentage is the highest ever by a Select Sires proven sire and remains close to the top in the breed today. Groves View Agenda Tina ET, bred by the Groves family in Billings, Mo., may be one of AGENDA's most esteemed daughters and exemplifies the type of genetics Select Sires is passionate about developing for the breed. She is not only a sixth generation Excellent scored "2E93," but she also just made a 365-day lactation of 34,879 Milk, 1,699 Fat and 1,202 Protein." –Adam Oswalt

7BS750 Hilltop Acres En DYNASTY ET *TM

"Fifteen years after his debut, DYNASTY has become the most widely used Brown Swiss bull in Select Sires' long history. He is the sire of nearly 200 daughters scored Excellent (90) or better, including notable show winners, All-American winners, top production cows and A.I. bull dams. However, most were, and continue to

7BS750 Hilltop Acres En DYNASTY

be, great milk cows that are profitable and enjoyable to have in any herd. Open rib, wide, flat rumps, high milk yield and low calving ease are accolades DYNASTY is known for contributing to the Brown Swiss breed. It is significant to note that until DYNASTY's success, the most widely used sire at Select Sires was none other than his grandsire, 7BS674 Top Acres Elegant SIMON (VG-87), whose name is prominent in the Brown Swiss breed thanks in part to his sons, Jetway, Even and Ensign." –Adam Oswalt

Daughter of 7BS750 DYNASTY, Brothers Three Brandi

7BS752 Sun-Made Garbro PRESTIGE ET M*

7BS752 Sunmade Garbro PRESTIGE 2004

Daughter of 7BS752 PRESTIGE, JoDee Prestige Kaluwa

"As the Simon lineage began to dominate the breed's pedigrees, the outcross PRESTIGE was released as a Select Sires Super Sampler and returned to active service as a proven bull a few years later once his first-crop daughters proved to be high-producing cows with exceptional mammary systems. He would later sire the renowned Bail-Mik P Lady Liberty-ET "E91 E91MS," who firmly occupied the No. 1 PPR spot for continuous evaluations. Another notable daughter of PRESTIGE was the three-time All-American and three-time reserve All-American Jo-Dee Prestige Kaluwa "E94 E94MS", a beloved cow that competed for six consecutive years at World Dairy Expo. PRESTIGE is the only bull to sire a No. 1 PPR cow and an Excellent (94) cow. He has truly lived up to his name and is considered one of Select Sires' best." -Adam Oswalt

GUERNSEY

7GU302 Rozelyn Pat Mar P GOLIATH-ET

7GU302 Rozelyn Pat Mar P GOLIATH

"GOLIATH has to be Select's real sleeper impact sire in the Guernsey breed! The bull was simply ahead of his time as the unmistakable source of longevity and health traits for the breed. I remember vividly being told by breeders that the GOLIATH's just didn't make enough milk as two-year-olds, weren't wide enough and had their pins up too high. Those reports were true but the attributes that GOLIATH provided are well documented today. His daughters had quality udders that lasted, produced high component milk, bred back and survived lactation after lactation. Today, GOLIATH, bred by Leon Zweegman, Lynden, Wash., is recognized as the breed's outlier for PL and DPR at high Reliability while offering a unique sire stack (Pat's Prince x Honor x Able) that has helped to maintain diversity." –Blaine Crosser

Daughter of 7GU302 GOLIATH, Abiqua Acres Goliath Velma

7GU360 Trotacre Loral TILLER-ET

"TILLER came to Select Sires as a replacement bull when the Guernsey Association wanted to syndicate my contract bull at the World Guernsey Conference and National Convention. The breeder, Jim Trotter, Enon Valley, Pa. offered TILLER as a substitute, which turned out great for Select and the Guernsey breed. TILLER was sired by 7GU322 Trotacre Mercury LORAL-ET, a promising unproven bull siring fancy show type out of a national class-leading two-year-old

7GU360 Trotacres Loral TILLER

"milk wagon" Magic daughter. The bull got the best traits of both of his parents, siring a consistent type pattern that provided outstanding strength and substance of bone, correct feet and legs and superior rear udders along with very good milk yield. TILLER was the Premier Sire at World Dairy Expo five consecutive years and even today will make an All-American nomination. No sire dominated the decade of the 2000s like TILLER!"-Blaine Crosser

Daughter of 7GU360 TILLER, Whitehall Tillers Barley

7GU395 Sniders Option AARON-ET

7GU395 Sniders Option Aaron

Daughter of 7GU395 AARON, Knapps Aaron Olivie

"AARON's legacy is still in the making as his sons receive their genetic proofs! At time of writing, AARON ranks as the breed's highest PTI sire with 98 percent Reliability and will likely only give up the top spot to one of his sons in the near future. AARON's dam made breed history when she was named grand champion at World Dairy Expo in 2000 because she was not a tall cow. Her terrific udder and balance made Altann (EX-95-EX-95-MS-GSD) the Guernsey cow everybody loved. AARON was a great source for fat test improvement and came at a time when the breed wanted to regain some lost components from years of emphasis on high milk production sires. Developed at Snider Homestead Farm by the Gable Family, New Enterprise, Pa., AARON has been recognized as a sire of moderate framed cattle with superior feet and legs and outstanding udders, earning him great customer satisfaction in the breed." -Blaine Crosser

High Impact Sires: L-R Front: 7HO8081 Planet, 7HO7872 Advent-Red, 7HO7004 Damion, 7HO6417 O Man. Center: 7HO5157 Durham, 7HO1897 Blackstar, 7HO5375 BW Marshall, 7HO5708 Blitz. Back: 7HO2236 Elton, 7HO477 Glendell, 7HO3948 Emory, 7HO980 Mark, 7HO543 Bell, 7HO58 Elevation.

The dairy bulls represented in these pages are just a sampling of the tremendous genetic impact that Select Sires has offered to the customers of the cooperative for 50 years. The sire group represented here and the group featured in the 25-year history book of Select Sires have populated the genetics of their individual breeds more than any other AI company and the influence is growing. In 2007, Select Sires commissioned the "Impact Sires of the Breed" artwork featuring Select Sires legends 7HO1057 Regancrest Elton DURHAM (EX-90-GM), 7HO3948 MJR Blackstar EMORY (EX-97-GM), 7HO2236 Emprise Bell ELTON (EX-95), 7HO5375 Mara-Thon BW MARSHALL (VG-86-GM), 7HO5708 Fustead Emory BLITZ-ET (EX-95-GM), 7HO1897 To-Mar BLACKSTAR-ET (EX-93-GM), 7HO980 Walkway Chief MARK (VG-87-GM), 7HO477 GLENDELL Arlinda Chief (EX-93-GM), 7HO543 Carlin-M Ivanhoe BELL (EX-93-GM) and 7HO58 Round Oak Rag Apple ELEVATION (EX-96-GM). In 2013, the artwork was updated to recognize four additional Select Sires greats in 7HO8081 Ensenada Taboo PLANET-ET (EX-90-GM), 7HO7872 KHW Kite ADVENT-RED-ET (EX-94), 7HO7004 Erbacres DAMION (EX-96) and 7HO6417 O-Bee MANfred Justice-ET (EX-94-GM).

Countless features in every dairy breed have populated breed publications, newsletters, and promotional materials. In the era before genomics the connection that the

Select Sires sire analyst had to the breeder was the key reason that many of these legends ended up at Select Sires. At the sire committee meeting just before the 50th anniversary of Select Sires, a committee member asked if the genomic era has or will impact the ability of Select Sires to continue to attract the great sires of the breed. The following story was relayed as yet another example of the Select Sires team using a network of talented people to attract great sires to the company. The story involves how 7HO11314 Mountfield SSI DCY MOGUL-ET ended up at Select Sires. MOGUL almost made the inclusion of sire write-ups for this history edition but his story is still being written and he will best be covered in the next edition.

In the words of Rick VerBeek, here is how MOGUL ended up coming to Select Sires. It is an example of why cow families will always remain important to Select Sires. "I think there is actually a nice "story" behind all of this. The key points really are that an SMS evaluator (John Erbsen, when picturing) told me to go back and check out Moguls grand dam years before. She was a LITTLE (53 inches) two year old, but calved a 2nd time with an amazing udder and it became easy to contract her, however before that could happen, she was sold to De-Su. John again called when he pictured the Marsh, very fresh, to say how nice she was. I followed up from there. The decision to use Dorcy at the time was because I loved Bret Daffers and wanted to use her son as much as possible. We commented about how we believe it is still very important to see cows in the genomic era. If I wasn't so familiar with Bret Daffers, I might not have been so aggressive in using Dorcy early on." In an era when numbers carry a lot of weight and there is less separation between "numbers", cow families and good cattle will always remain the focus of Select Sires.

6

◆ ◆ ◆

The Meat of the Situation

◆ ◆ ◆

In corporate America, many publicly traded companies take precautions to stay nimble and not become such a large behemoth of a company that they lose focus of their purpose or the ability to innovate. A review of Select Sires shows how the cooperative structure strives to maintain programs that continue to meet a niche in serving the membership and as a proving ground for new services and research. The Select Sires beef program is one of those areas of influence. The semen sales of Select Sires has been predominantly dairy sire sales; in 1966 beef unit sales reflected 16 percent of the overall sales of the federation. In 1990, beef sales were 8 percent of overall unit sales and in 2014 beef breed sires contributed 6 percent of the overall unit sales. A casual observer could look at those figures and come to the conclusion that beef is not a very important part of the Select Sires product line. That would be a severe underestimation of the situation.

The Select Sires beef department has been a key proving ground for innovations that have gone on to benefit all members of the cooperative including young sire sampling, synchronization protocol research and online semen ordering. When you add the involvement that Select Sires has had with the Beef Improvement Federation (BIF), that same casual observer will quickly notice that the influence of the Select Sires beef department goes far beyond the unit sales. It is also important to add that the percentage

Roy Wallace was the architect of the Select Sires beef program, working with beef leaders to implement Structured Sire Evaluation programs, Frame Scores, Power Scores, and DNA marker usage for the industry.

drop of overall sales is more a reflection of growth in the dairy market rather than loss in the beef market as Select Sires has grown from selling 136,907 units of beef semen in 1966 to 764,782 in 2014; over a five-fold increase.

That sales growth is a reflection of many of the programs mentioned in this chapter and many of the recurring themes in this book; programs focused on the member, led by good people with the best intentions of the member in focus. A review of the good people that have been involved in the Select Sires beef program has to begin with Roy Wallace. Wallace began with COBA/Select Sires Inc., in 1967 after being an active student as an Ohio State Buckeye. In 1969, he joined Select Sires Inc., staff as beef sire analyst. He was later promoted to vice president, beef programs and oversaw the acquisition of 600 beef bulls in 19 different breeds during his tenure.

Just as the birth of ELEVATION and Select Sires coinciding in 1965, Wallace beginning his career in 1967 just as the BIF was initiated was equally significant. The BIF began at an organizational meeting on January 12, 1968 in Denver, Colo. just as Wallace was getting his start in the industry. From the very first BIF convention to the 2007 convention, Wallace never missed a BIF gathering and his involvement in the group and guiding the beef program at Select Sires helped both organizations bring key guidance to the beef industry. Wallace was a catalyst in introducing Expected Progeny Difference (EPD) calculations, Structured Sire Evaluation programs, Frame Scores, Power Scores (precursors for today's $Value Indexes), utilization of ultrasound information for carcass merit and DNA marker usage to the industry. He also led the charge to improve estrus synchronization programs and worked to insure that the programs were user friendly. Much of this work is still relevant in the industry and at Select Sires today.

It is interesting to review the growth of the beef program at Select Sires and see the course that the beef department took in serving the membership. A review of the early annual reports of the cooperative shows a desire to establish Select Sires as a true player on the national level. Thus much of the emphasis early on was centered on a presence at national livestock shows and expositions and consistently being represented with people and marketing materials. Around the mid-1980s, the course moved to establishing an identity for the Select Sires beef program. Select Sires was accepted as a company that

7AN178 BAR Ext

would be around for the long haul and a move towards the type of sire that Select Sires would be known for in the marketplace, carcass merit type sires was made. These cattle that were valued based on their performance, not on how they looked, fit the goals of the cooperative. Not coincidentally, three straight annual reports in the mid-1980s used almost the same paragraph to describe the state of the industry as "one of low beef prices causing a decrease in unit sales but an increase in dollars generated." This was summarized as a movement of the Select Sires beef customer to the purebred type of sire.

As the 1980s drew to a close and the company moved into the 1990s, a few things were noticeable. One was that the beef department was not afraid to try new marketing techniques in order to reach the customer. Reports continually spoke of record sales and continued growth in the marketplace. The late 1980s witnessed major herd liquidations in the industry and the industry poised for growth. To capitalize on this growth, Select Sires produced a beef video beginning in 1987 that served as a convenient delivery method for many years to educate employees and customers about the headliners in the beef lineup. Narrated by Wallace, the video production even transitioned to satellite production for a few years to take advantage of that medium. Another concept that started to take off in beef circles in the early 1990s was the use of reproductive tools in helping beef customers to achieve excellent conception rates. Products such as Synchromate-B became available, allowing Select Sires customers a new method for getting

7AN222 PREDESTINED

semen into both heifers and cows. It was the beginning of much additional research for convenient semen delivery projects for all breeds.

The 1990s also introduced a stronger focus on research, training and education in the beef department at Select Sires. More emphasis was placed on an annual beef tour to allow employees of the cooperative to see offspring of Select Sires bulls in member herds. It also allowed the customer-owners of the cooperative to have an audience with the beef department and the people selling the bulls; a valuable opportunity for true member feedback. In-house at Select Sires, a fall beef synchronization research gathering grew into a larger collection of university researchers and professors. Synchronization protocols such as Select Synch and work with melengestrol acetate (MGA) feed additive for simplifying synchronization on beef females came out of this gathering of industry leaders. The importance of this research cannot be overestimated. Feeding a hungry world requires more output from less input. This synchronization research has allowed more animals to be inseminated with top genetic A.I. sires while requiring less labor and inputs than ever before. As the new millennium began, beef at Select Sires took on a new direction by reaching customers through digital sources. A rancher could now sit on his horse with a smartphone dialed into www.selectsiresbeef.com and administer the protocol required for this time saving innovation.

Select Sires beef sales were on a roll and it appeared that the structure was in place to

The annual beef tour takes Select Sires representatives around the country to learn the needs of different styles of production. These representatives can then use this education to advise the beef customers in the areas that they serve.

continue this momentum. Then 2008 arrived and some major changes rocked the Select Sires beef program. In January, Wallace passed away while attending one of the premier events in the industry and his sudden passing was a tremendous loss not only for Select Sires, but for the beef industry. Wallace was the leader of the beef program for 40 years and his death while at the National Western Stock Show in Denver marked the end of an era along with the beginning of a new one. The loss of Wallace and newly discovered genetic recessives in the Angus breed, in the same year created immense challenges for the program. The beef program utilized ideas from members and the Select Sires family to focus efforts on the customers to better fulfill their wants and needs. The years of experience possessed by several employees at the member level was vital during this time and member input was the impetus for carrying on with a renewed focus and direction.

Technology truly has guided the beef department's direction over the last 10 years, but it has also presented challenges that did not previously exist. Recessive genes are one example. The ability to dig deeper into the sequence of the bovine genome provided the ability to find information that was always there, but couldn't be seen. It has been equivalent to a detective acquiring a stronger magnifying glass to find the clues. One of the first discoveries that occurred was a genetic defect in the Angus breed, Arthrogryposis Multiplex (AM) in 2008. Select Sires and the industry no longer had to wait for the physical identification of offspring to identify an animal as a carrier of a recessive gene. Testing available to breeders of female and male offspring could identify the carriers and non-carriers of a recessive in the herd. Breed guidelines then gave direction as to how the recessive can be managed.

AM hit Select Sires quite extensively with many sires being affected and a second recessive, Neuropathic Hydrocephalus (NH) was identified in 2009, creating a double whammy on the Angus lineup. Combined with many economic uncertainties around the world in 2009, it was tough for the Select Sires beef program to manage. It truly was a crossroads for the program and all options were on the table, including terminating the program. After much discussion it was decided that a cooperative serving its membership should strive to provide good options in all species and breeds, especially given the momentum that the beef department had going before the discovery of the recessives. Additional investments were committed to the program and 18 new Angus bulls joined the lineup in 2009 from a variety of sources. It was a renewed commitment to the beef program and its ability to serve the membership while also providing an agile incubator within the larger company to foster ideas and research.

In 2009 Select Sires launched a new beef website (www.selectsiresbeef.com). For the first time Select Sires had a dedicated website that allowed online semen ordering. It also provided current information about the lineup of beef sires, featured video clips of sires and progeny, provided a searchable sire sort for each breed and included breeder cattle classifieds. It has become a go-to location for relevant beef information and has introduced new customers to the power of the Select Sires beef lineup. Since beef marketing behaves differently than dairy marketing (due to the frequency of evaluations), the way A.I. certificates are ordered and the focus of A.I. timing in certain parts of the year, the beef website has provided an excellent resource for employees and customers alike to acquire the information needed for A.I. success.

The success of the beef program does share a strong connection to the success of the dairy program and the fact is that success ultimately starts with a pregnancy. Just as dairy customers have benefited from the increased reproductive expertise up and down the Select Sires staff, beef customers have benefited from investing in additional personnel trained to meet their reproductive needs. This includes technicians trained in the expertise of managing synchronization projects, Select Sires beef specialists and independent beef specialists that supplement the service efforts of member cooperative staff. With the focus of beef breeding occurring in a few seasons of the year, "synch projects" have sprung up across the country allowing customers the ability to utilize Select Sires technician service in new ways. The customer can identify a set of females to be inseminated and turn the entire group over to trained staff in a turnkey approach. The technician discusses the projects with the customer, identifies the methods that may work for that individual farm and executes the plan with what has been exceptional results. Tools such as reproductive hormones or CIDRs that may seem daunting to a customer only breeding animals a few times a year, can be easily implemented because of this expertise. Select Sires beef specialists and independent beef representatives can also fill needs for beef customers. Beef specialists are a group of beef-focused Select Sires employees that serve as an excellent connection between the beef department at headquarters and the local member cooperative staff. This is another example of a train-the-trainer approach, allowing additional information to reach the member. Independent beef representatives function in much the same way, allowing additional reach for the beef department to customers of the cooperative. This group of individuals have strong beef interest but are not employed directly by Select Sires and are able to provide sales and service to a larger geographic area.

The team of beef specialists and independent beef representatives are supported by the beef department staff in many unique ways. Brian House joined Select Sires in 1991 and offers support for the overall beef program and services that help beef customers. Aaron Arnett, Ph.D., is the beef genetics manager, devoting his time to sire analysis and procuring the best beef sires for the program. He has been working in that capacity since 2008. Since being named public relations and communications coordinator in 2010, Luke Bowman developed novel methods of social media and training methods for spreading the news of the exciting developments in the Select Sires beef program to the member-owners. It is a growing method for getting real-time information about beef developments within Select Sires.

As one looks at the future of the Select Sires beef department, there are some new developments already beginning to emerge that will allow for additional service to the membership. One of these is the "beef on dairy" philosophy already being seen in the Breeding to Feeding program. As genomic technology has allowed dairy producers to get an even more accurate prediction on the performance capabilities of their replacement herd, Select Sires has developed tools to help producers identify which animals are best suited for seed stock and which animals will provide maximum economic return at the terminal market. Inventory management tools help to identify the animal for use in the Breeding to Feeding program allowing the dairy animals to be bred to a LimFlex® or a Limousin sire, available through a partnership with the Wulf Cattle Company, to maximize return on the calf. The Breeding to Feeding program provides a premium price at purchase, but beef can be the best decision on some dairy animals even if the Breeding to Feeding program is not utilized and Select Sires has developed inventory tools to calculate the return for the customer.

Another trend that looks to continue in the future is Select Sires aligning with key seedstock sources for developing sires that fit the marketplace. Breeding establishments such as Gardiner Angus Ranch, Kansas, Wehrmann Angus, Virginia, and Deer Valley, Tennessee, have carried a strong following in the Angus breed. By working with these producers to create sires to fit the marketplace, Select Sires produces a consistent lineup of productive sires and customers know what to expect from offspring.

The mantra of the Select Sires beef program is Conception, Calving ease, Carcass and Cows. Most breeders agree that a sire program delivering those four attributes will be well on the way to becoming a trusted supplier for the farm. Select Sires continues to

7AN194 RITO 616

Fred Stivers

SELECT SIRES

rely on a beef sire committee of customer-owners to provide feedback on the program.

Investments in the Select Sires beef program have provided a return to the membership and that return has translated to growth. In the first year of operations, Select Sires sold 136,000 units of beef semen and 25 years later that total had grown to 380,000 units. Today over 1 million units of semen from beef sires are sold each year. Growth can bring growing pains. One of the challenges with growing the beef program is keeping semen production ahead of sales. As demand for stall space in Plain City grew and beef sales continued to grow, the need to have a facility to house beef bulls grew with it. Because of these space restrictions, Prairie State/Select Sires remodeled their facility in 2012 to house beef bulls. This facility now houses around 40 beef bulls at any given time and has become a place where semen production and semen quality has been improved. The appearance of beef bulls that live there is fantastic and the bulls are accessible to both the sales team and to the public. In terms of impact on the beef program and having enough product to meet the growing demand throughout the world, the housing of beef bulls at Prairie State has been extremely beneficial. Customer-owners are reaping the rewards from this move to Illinois with more available product than they have had in years on a wider variety of bulls.

Select Sires is best known for its dairy program and dairy sires but the beef program has provided much more to the cooperative than just 6 percent of unit sales. By being a smaller, agile segment of Select Sires, the beef department has been able to innovate and introduce many programs and research projects within Select Sires that all would recognize. It is just one more way that the cooperative model serves the individual well.

IMPACT BEEF SIRES

Following are thoughts from Brian House, beef program and product manager for Select Sires on some of the more influential beef bulls: "Nearly all of the high unit sales bulls from the beef program have earned their rank in the most recent 25 years. The list of high-sellers is lengthy, but some of the more notable ones can definitely be called impact bulls. Select Sires' all-time record high-selling beef bull is 7AN194 RITO 6I6 who made his name by consistently delivering low birth weights and extremely gentle dispositions. During the same period of time, 7AN178 BAR EXT was housed in the same barn with 6I6 and ended up as our No. 2 bull for unit sales. His ability to deliver calving ease along with beautiful daughters with near-perfect udders helped propel him to this position. Both 6I6 and BAR EXT were able to take advantage of a period when heifer A.I. was growing and some of the previously mentioned synchronization protocols were gaining in popularity. Several other bulls deserve recognition for their accomplishments, most notably 7AN222 PREDESTINED, who was recognized as the highest $B bull in the Angus breed for a period of years when this trait was first introduced. Following PREDESTINED, 7AN80 AMBUSH ranks as the No. 4 all-time unit sales beef bull and during his peak years, AMBUSH made up nearly 25 percent of our Angus sales. 7AN100 TRAVELER 5204, known for calving ease and superior udders, 7AN133 RAINMAKER 814Z, outcross and calving ease sire, 7AN95 SCOTCH CAP, the carcass king and 7AN92 BIG SKY, show bull of the year for several years, were all famous in their own right, each delivering what our customers demanded, better beef cattle. The Angus breed has always been our high-selling breed, making up from 70 to 85 percent of our total beef sales in a given year. So, you would expect our high selling bulls to be Angus bulls. Two non-Angus bulls that reached the 100,000 unit plateau during their careers at Select Sires were 7BR517 817/3 and 7AR40 VIRILE. 817/3 was a favorite with the barn crew because he lived at headquarters until he was 17-years-old!"

7

Maximizing Production from the Herd

I t is sometimes easy to overlook the fact that Select Sires' production facilities are still dairy and beef operations. Chief Executive Officer David Thorbahn often introduces himself as the manager of a 2,000-head farm and the same challenges and standard operating procedures that other dairy and beef farms face are also in play at Select Sires. Animals get sick, crop production is affected by the weather and nutrients must be managed. It takes a team to make it work and the smarter the people on that team, the better the results.

As any farm or company grows, jobs that were previously outsourced can be brought in- house for the benefit of efficiency and economy of scale. Dr. Don Monke was the first to hold one of these in-house positions at Select Sires. In the first few years of the fledgling A.I. company, the work was steady but not steady enough to justify a full-time in-house veterinarian. Thus the leaders of the cooperative contracted with the best large-animal veterinarian that they knew of, Dr. Harrison Gardner from The Ohio State University who also worked as the veterinarian for the Columbus Zoo. As the enterprise grew, the decision was made that the high-value sires residing at Select Sires needed their own caretaker that would be able to monitor performance, attend to medical needs and ensure that the care and health of the bulls was at an optimum level on a daily basis.

The time had come to hire Dr. Monke. Monke grew up on a beef and swine farm in Mt. Olive, Ill. As a youngster helping out on the family farm, one of his first chores was to stand on the fence and observe for heats. His interest in animals led him to know that he wanted to be involved with taking care of animals from an early age and he went to the University

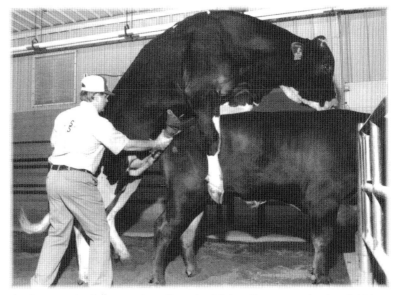

The first step in the processing of a unit of Select Sires semen begins right here in the collection arena.

of Illinois for his biological science and veterinarian doctorate degrees graduating No. 1 in his class in 1977, as the youngest person in his class. At the same time Select Sires advertised for an in-house veterinarian position. This caught Dr. Monke's interest, he applied and was selected from four applicants as the first staff veterinarian for Select Sires. Along the way there have been eight veterinarians that have served on the staff at Select Sires including the current staff of three full-time veterinarians plus Dr. Monke.

The veterinarian position remained relatively unchanged until 1982 when the first assistant veterinarian position was added. In 1989, Howard Kellgren retired as the long-time director of production at Select Sires. This was an opportunity to split up responsibilities to better handle the tremendous growth that had occurred. At this time, Dale Pennington was named vice president of production services, Clif Marshall was named vice president of semen quality and research and Dr. Monke was named vice president of sire health programs.

Keeping a bull healthy and productive has not changed much from when Select Sires first started. Sure, there is additional research on nutrition and herd health but the main concept of keeping an animal healthy remains very much the same. What has changed is having a system in place that can handle sire health with standard operating procedures. At the time of Dr. Monke's hiring, he commented that the biggest thing was getting to know 300 bulls and keeping track of their names and numbers. As the herd size of Select Sires grew to closer to 2,000, it became much more a system of implementing procedures that were followed to ensure optimum health for the bulls and to qualify for each of the different countries where Select Sires semen is in demand.

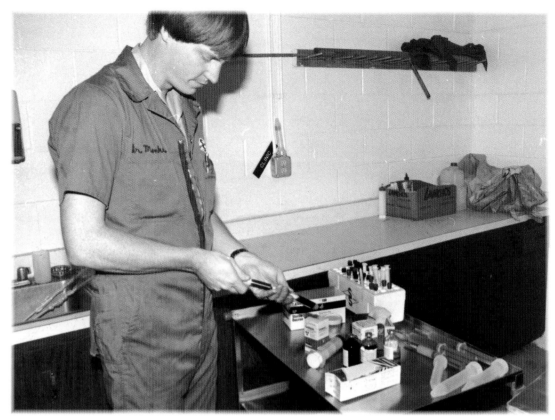

Dr. Don Monke, staff veterinarian since 1977 prepares testing materials for a sire health evaluation.

As a first-year veterinarian at Select Sires, Dr. Monke oversaw exports that saw 3 to 4 percent of total production leave the United States. Today the figure is closer to 30 percent. Record keeping in the early days required a few papers a week, today 50 percent of the job is to ensure that all regulations are followed, all health tests are administered and that all semen that leaves Select Sires is exactly what the purchaser expects in genetics and quality. A positive outcome that has happened over the last 20 years is that some consistency has been found in the requirements and standards for each individual country. In the 1980s, each country had their own standards. In some cases, it was to protect the health of the home herd but in many cases it was by design to protect the markets of the domestic A.I. centers. One country would come up with a hoop to jump through for semen export and the next country would copy that hoop with a wrinkle of their own. It was a game of seeing who could outdo the others.

In the early 1990s, Dr. Monke traveled with a National Association of Animal Breeders (NAAB) delegation to Brussels as the consulting veterinarian to standardize the guidelines for semen production around the world. It was a big step towards simplifying the process of semen production and opened some markets for breeders around the world to utilize the genetics of Select Sires. It was not without challenges however. As part of the negotiations, the European Union (EU) and world markets moved from a system that would allow individual bulls to qualify for export to a system where the whole herd of an A.I. center must qualify for export. This added to the difficulty of qualifying bulls for sale around the globe but it was a logical move from a health standpoint.

In 1983, a fruitful market for genetics opened up in Japan. Japan now has a vibrant dairy industry and a lot of it can be attributed to an NAAB delegation that visited the country. Representatives from different U.S. A.I. companies traveled to Japan to look at the genetic guidelines and health conditions that they would require for their A.I. program. Negotiations were productive and the Japanese market has always been a strong market for World Wide Sires sales. Interestingly, Japan has a requirement for stature in their bulls and they receive the hip height for every sire that is in their program. They are the only country in the world to do so. Another notable export opening was the Soviet Union agreeing to buy semen from Select Sires in 1985. This occurred after a delegation, including Dr. Monke, traveled to the country to negotiate production and genetic standards.

To meet the needs and health requirements of different A.I. markets, different buildings and production areas must be constructed. Many of the building projects at Select Sires have been planned for current market demands with future market growth in mind. Dr. Monke has been in charge of most of the recent building projects at Select Sires, many of which have won awards or been featured in the farm press for their innovation and efficiency. He credits the team that he works with at Select Sires for designing functional buildings that add to efficiency. When you go from producing 6 million units of semen to 14 million units of semen in a very short time on a building area that is roughly the same footprint, efficiencies were achieved.

One example is the construction of the dry goods building storage facility at headquarters. By working with input from Bill Delong, maintenance supervisor, the production team realized that expanding the ceiling to 14 feet would provide another 2,500 square feet of semen storage capacity in the remaining building. The decision to go vertical for products that could be stored in a vertical system gave much needed production space.

Other projects reflect the same efficiency and adaptation of current building advancements. The former dry cow barn at the Hecker Facility was converted to 14 box stalls to start and later an additional 14 box stalls were added for a total of 28. This was essentially "found space" that helped to meet the demand for additional semen and sires at Select Sires. Another big project was the export barns on what is called the McKitrick Farm, so named because it was purchased from the McKitrick family. That farm was purchased November 30, 2009 and to minimize any tax effects from the transaction, new barns had to be in place within six months. So, planning had begun before the purchase was completed. Dr. Monke designed the blueprints for the facility, Todd Eades, bull movement coordinator, designed the collection facility and Delong designed the utilities including the electricity and plumbing. Hochstetler Buildings Inc. was contracted to build the barns and the project was completed by Memorial Day 2010. It was a tremendous

The bright lights of the Kellgren Center signify to a sire that they have made it to the big time with Select Sires.

achievement and another example of people coming together to make things happen; even more notable was that most of the work had to be completed during winter. These new barns were important because prior to completion, Select Sires had been using two barns in the Hecker Center for most EU production. Federal veterinarians observing the collection process expressed that it would be necessary in the future to not have any cross contamination of people or equipment between facilities in order to keep bulls qualified for an EU environment.

These new barns allowed Select Sires to create facilities where the people and equipment were dedicated to only being used in their isolated environments. Each barn gave Select Sires 44 new stalls, which were needed for growth and between the new barns 80 sires and eight mount animals joined the production group. Barn E1 is used to isolate proven sires for the EU and the sires change after each sire summary. Barn E2 was originally dedicated to the four-year-old program, collecting semen in advance of a bull getting his sire summary. Today that barn is closer to 50 percent four-year-old bulls and 50 percent Super Sampler sires, reflecting the growth in demand for those young sires. Brian Spires was the first supervisor of those barns and has led production efforts to accomplish 3 million units of production annually from those barns. A fitting accomplishment considering the population turns over so often in those facilities.

Shortly after the EU facility project the Aggressive Reproductive Technologies™ (ART™) program was taking off and the decision was made to develop a calf campus. The design phase began in the first half of 2011, construction began that June and Select Sires began using the new facility in the fall of 2011. It was needed to house the valuable calves being produced by the ART program bringing calves into Select Sires at a younger age from breeders. The discovery that lifetime semen production could be enhanced by beginning calves on a designed nutrition and health plan at an early age validated the need for the calf campus. Select Sires worked with Dr. Ken Nordlund from the University of Wisconsin to study ventilation and its effect on health of young bovines. Dr. Nordlund provided all of the new research on ventilation and Select Sires implemented most of it into the new facilities. The innovation and resulting performance from the calf campus garnered quite a bit of positive attention from the press and has even been recognized with awards for innovation and effective housing methods.

Most importantly there has been very minimal death loss from the facilities. Staff veterinarian, Dr. Liz Lahmers takes it as her personal crusade to not lose any calves and the performance has been remarkable. One special note is that in the era before genomics, a calf was selected at the farm based on being the biggest, strongest, healthiest calf in the group. With genomics and today's movement towards a more moderately sized animal, we are not always getting the biggest, strongest calf. This has the potential to create problems for survivability of calves but there has not been any additional loss. If anything, survival rates are better with genomic selection than they were previously and the calves thrive with the optimal living conditions and care that they receive.

Other notable sire management changes at Select Sires includes the implementation of the "all in-all out" protocol introduced by Dr. Bill Ayers in the early 2000s. In the first month of each quarter bulls are grouped together to start them on the protocols that they will go through at Select Sires at the time. Deb Trimble manages that process and groups the sires for proper standard operating procedures.

In 2005, Jim Pond was named bull nutrition supervisor. The decision was made at that point to go away from feeding individual ingredients to a total mixed ration (TMR). In the first six to 12 months the number of displaced abomasums (DAs) moved from 12 to 13 per year to zero, or maybe one per year. That keeps bulls on production and their semen available for the customers that demand it. In the pursuit of producing 15 million units per year, positive changes like that can make a big difference. Select Sires raises all of its own corn silage and approximately one-third of the hay that is fed. It is tested, and then by working with other nutrition companies, additional feed supplements are developed to complement the forages raised on the farm. At six to eight months of age, the sires are placed on a growth ration to achieve 2 to 2.5 pounds of growth per day towards mature weight. Once the desired mature size is achieved, a maintenance ration is implemented to keep bulls at a proper body condition score (BCS). Sires are appraised

Dr. Liz Lahmers, staff veterinarian, conducting health testing on bulls at Select Sires.

for their BCS four times a year to ensure that they are not getting too fat and that they remain lean for optimal health and semen production.

Dairy bulls respond well to adjustments in feed for body maintenance. Beef bulls present a different challenge due to the way they mobilize energy for fat. The beef program has continued to grow at Select Sires and additional fine-tuning has been implemented to maximize the semen production of beef sires. Moving some of these sires to Prairie State/Select Sires' semen collection has enabled additional grouping of sires in similar production systems.

At headquarters a name that has been synonymous with semen production at the Kellgren Center is Barry Slack. Slack was the original supervisor of production at the facility when it began operating in mid-1988 until his retirement in 2014. His time with Select Sires echoes that of many other employees in that he spent his entire career working for the cooperative. Beginning employment in 1974 as a herdsman on the night crew, Barry later became one of the original herdsmen at the sire-in-waiting group-housing facility. He began working on the headquarters collection crew in 1978 before becoming supervisor in mid-1988 with the new facility.

As manager of the Kellgren Center, Slack and his crew were responsible for the collection of over 90 million straws of semen. In 2003, Slack also was named manager of the

Hecker Center, which was a logical promotion given that Kellgren and Hecker were the Select Sires EU-approved facilities at the time. Straw production at the Hecker Center under Slacks's supervision was an additional 25 million straws of semen. This means that he has been the supervisor for over 120 million straws of semen and the crews that collected it for over 25 years.

While those are remarkable totals, Barry is quick to credit the Select Sires way; stating that he and his crew were always simply striving to do their best. "It is truly a team effort of outstanding people achieving outstanding results," he said. "Every member of the federation must be recognized because these numbers were a result of the law of supply and demand, which dictated that our collection crews optimize the abilities to harvest an optimum quantity of semen from each bull."

Gregg Marsh is another long-time employee of Select Sires that has delivered the future for the federation by overseeing the collection of 4 million straws of Program for Genetic Advancement (PGA) semen annually. Young sires in the PGA have erratic production schedules and abilities. Coordination of that collection is crucial to delivering the young sire semen to the field for use in a timely basis to maximize genetic progress. On the proven end of things, Elmer Watkins has managed the Wells Road Facility and the sires that live there which are not approved for international shipment. Sires such as BW MARSHALL, EMORY and DURHAM called that facility home and were a big part of the success of Select Sires.

With the acquisition of Sire Power in 2000, their collection facilities and sire housing added to the capacity for production at Select Sires. Semen was processed at the Pennsylvania facility until May 4, 2004 at which point a study of the economies of scale showed that consolidation of all collections in Ohio would provide a good return to the membership. Sires remain housed at the Ebersole Valley View Complex in Tunkhannock, Pa. There supervisor, Butch Sands, and farm manager, Bob Fetterow, work with a team that oversees 380 box stalls housing 365 sires-in-waiting.

As for the future of sire housing and production, genomic information has helped selection intensity and Select Sires sampled 250 Holstein bulls in 2014 as compared to 330 Holstein bulls in 2009. That 80-bull difference equates to a need for 300 less stalls if the trend holds over time. This allows the production managers at Select Sires to do the same thing that a milking dairy herd manager would do; arrange animals for less crowding and maximize results with more space available for production. At the same time the Jersey program is growing from 40 sires to 70 sires meaning that 120 of the stalls are already reserved for additions to the Jersey program.

The extra housing capacity at Select Sires has also allowed fewer bulls to reside in group housing. In 1977 sires were being graduated to the active lineup from group housing, meaning that a five-year-old bull might have come from group housing. Today

Each month, well over 1 million units are produced at Select Sires and shipped to customers around the world.

the oldest bull in group housing is around two-years-old. This creates a safer environment and allows for a smoother transition for a bull going from an in-waiting status to active status.

An additional challenge for the future is one that affects every large animal production operation, environmental and nutrient resource management. Since the mid-2000s the environmental program at Select Sires has become a major area of focus. Training and compliance programs for employees have been developed and implemented to be at the forefront of what the community and government expect from a leading company. The product produced by Select Sires is unique and thus there are very few industry programs available to train a person working with what is produced in Plain City, Ohio. Whereas a bank could send an employee for training put on by some government entity, Select Sires has to develop many of the protocols and much of the training on their own to prepare employees for doing things the right way in a responsible manner with bull handling, nutrient management, tractor driving and many of the other unique aspects of the industry.

With a herd of over 2,000 large animals, manure management is a key focus of the enterprise. Self-sufficiency will be a key in the future because mulch companies that used to pay for the manure have moved to where they want to be paid for taking the product.

This means that Select Sires invests dollars and time in technology that can utilize more of the waste products produced by the animals. For example, a manure dryer that converts manure to a product that can be used half for energy and half for bedding provides a useful solution that benefits both ends of the semen production process.

Dairy and beef operations in the U. S. have grown in size and their expertise in handling that growth must grow along with them. Select Sires is no different. From the days of a few shared bulls at each member cooperative to today's large consolidated herd, Select Sires has developed training and techniques that keep animals healthy, maximize production and are responsible to the community and environment. That may sound like any other progressive, growing production agriculture facility and it does describe Select Sires at its core.

8

• • •

It All Starts with a Pregnancy

• • •

To earn a nickname in your professional career, you really have to do something that stands out among your peers and do it consistently. Babe Ruth earned the nickname "Sultan of Swat" for his propensity to hit home runs. The 40th President of the United States, Ronald Reagan, earned the nickname "The Great Communicator" for his ability to reach people with powerful words. So when you earn the nickname "Dr. Discard," there is a good chance that there is an excellent story behind that moniker. That story is part of why Select Sires has been a popular choice of the people for 50 years.

In the early days of A.I., quality control meant capturing the entire product without spilling it and hoping that no dirt got mixed in with the product while doing it. It was a fledgling technology that was not yet advanced enough to focus on tweaking and adjustments that could help boost the results. Fresh semen was more forgiving and the market had not reached a point where adjustments had to be made to the semen to maximize volume. It was a simpler product for a simpler time. The focus of genetics in the late 1960s was on improved conformation and production. The universal mantra for fertility has always been that it only takes one sperm cell to make a pregnancy so long as there was a sperm cell in the dose of semen; the cow had a chance to become pregnant.

As time went on, a chance was no longer good enough. Demanding breeders wanted a good likelihood that the animal would become pregnant. It didn't need to be possible, it should be probable that a unit of semen would get the job done the first time. It was obvious that research and testing needed to be done.

The early years of Select Sires were not easy and really were only a shell of what the company has become today. Financially challenged companies can't always dedicate the people, time or resources it takes to

The calendar on the wall confirms that 1954 was still a time of research with dry ice and alcohol semen freezing and storage.

deliver an elite product. However there comes a time when a company that hopes to see tomorrow has to make changes today. It is a sink-or-swim moment when a company puts the financial well-being of its customers ahead of its own in the hope of prospering in the future. If done correctly it will set a corporate philosophy that guides the company for the future. Many a company has missed that opportunity and entered anonymity because they ceased to exist. Select Sires chose to make fertility a hallmark and that continues to serve the company and the member-owners well in today's dairy and beef environment.

Clif Marshall, the aforementioned "Dr. Discard" for his commitment to throw away semen that does not reach the highest of standards, is one of the researchers that has been affiliated with Select Sires and the member cooperatives that form Select Sires for a long time. In fact, he and Howard Kellgren of Select Sires literally wrote the book on A.I. training, semen processing and optimizing fertility for the bovine species. Marshall has been internationally recognized for work done during his master's degree program validating the use of differential interference contrast (DIC) optics for evaluating the acrosomal membrane integrity of sperm cells. That high-level description essentially means that fertility is going to be enhanced when we can look at the make up of spermatozoa and connect it to the ability of an egg to be fertilized. The simpler point is that it works and it became the standard for semen evaluation throughout the world.

Marshall's career with Select Sires began in 1968 with Virginia Artificial Breeding Association. There he had many different roles: he collected bulls two days a week, supervised 13 technicians two days a week and drove the truck route delivering semen one day of the week. It was hands-on training for everything that the developing field of artificial insemination could deliver.

Clif Marshall stands with Sexing Technologies lab manager Candis McCleary in front of the Gender SELECTed semen facility in Ohio named in his honor.

The opportunity to process the product about 40 percent of the time and then go out and gauge the results 60 percent of the time was an ideal situation to observe performance and tweak the product where necessary, a real advantage for a young researcher learning the ropes.

"2000 Think Tank"

The Reproductive Physiology Think Tank is an outstanding opportunity for researchers across the globe to exchange ideas and create "better questions". This 2014 photo shows how it has grown.

When Virginia ABA joined Select Sires in 1969 and the sires from Virginia traveled to the Ohio and Michigan Select Sires processing facilities, it was evident that Marshall would travel with them to one of the locations. He ended up in Michigan, but financial challenges facing Select Sires dictated that production facilities should be combined at a central location. That central location would be Ohio and two years after moving to Michigan, Marshall would make the move with the bulls once again, this time to Ohio.

In Ohio, the financial challenges of Select Sires had led to the appointment of a new general manager, Jim Nichols. General Manager Nichols was concerned about the fertility of Select Sires semen and appointed Marshall as the first reproductive specialist for the cooperative. In this new role, Marshall would be responsible for taking A.I. training to a national level as well as developing the materials needed to make this relatively new technology easy to understand at the farm level. It was a precursor to the Select Reproductive Solutions (SRS) program and allowed Select Sires' customers and employees an opportunity to receive education beyond the original training of A.I. technique. Some of the training was one-on-one but there was also ample opportunity for education at annual meetings, extension meetings, and employee meetings. In the time before the internet and online training modules, this was the method for getting information disseminated.

A connection to education has always been a key for Select Sires, perhaps because the roots of many of the member cooperatives started in extension education. The list of university expertise that has helped Select Sires reads as a who's who of leading researchers and educators across the dairy and beef industries. Three that had exceptional influence on specific techniques and methods used at Select Sires include Clint Meadows, Ph.D., from Michigan State University who gave guidance on setting up the PGA young sire sampling system, John Almquist, Ph.D., from Penn State University who consulted on maximizing the sperm harvest efficiency of bulls, and Richard Saacke,

Ph.D., of Virginia Tech who wrote the book on the evaluation of semen quality and quality control. This research showed that a bull will produce 50 to 60 billion sperm cells per week, and it was up to Howard Kellgren and Clif Marshall to figure out how much of that could be put into usable straws.

In 1989, Kellgren retired and Marshall was named supervisor of processing for Select Sires. The Select Sires philosophy at that time was to operate in the leanest method possible. It worked for a year or so but after awhile it became evident that additional help and expertise was required. In 1990, Mel DeJarnette became available and was hired to assist in the production of semen and education on fertility at Select Sires. This continued a tradition of having a team in the production department that could research the latest semen production methods and implement the proven methods for improving fertility. The latest findings are taken to the field to train the Select Sires representatives on how their customers benefit from this research.

When asked how Select Sires has earned the reputation for top fertility in the semen realm, Marshall credits an attention to detail combined with the most effective post-thaw quality control system in the world as the main reasons for success. "Most semen production facilities in the world only use post-thaw motility as the post-production analysis," explains Marshall. "Select Sires uses four additional tests including morphology, incubator motility, and two flow cytometer evaluations to evaluate the potential fertility of the semen. One test tells you a little, five tests tell you a lot." DeJarnette has kept this research and evaluation going with additional research, most notably in new extenders and extender additives that have provided noticeable gains in generating additional pregnancies for Select Sires' member-owners.

The Program for Fertility Advancement™ (PFA™) has been one of the latest steps toward efficiently doing research and getting positive results into use for the members. DeJarnette mentions, "The PFA began shortly after David Thorbahn arrived and it formalized and efficiently benefitted what we have always done. Previously when we had a research project that we wanted to do, we would put out a notice to the member cooperatives, they would recruit participants and we would issue semen for the project. The problem with that method was that with new participants each time, we had to teach the proper ways to record data and track the research. Plus, some herds did not understand the need for quickly using the semen, so we would only end up with 50 percent of the data we expected and it would take 12 to 18 months to complete. PFA allowed us to identify herds that wanted to participate in as many trials as were available. These cooperator herds then understood what we expected from a data recording aspect while also using the research semen efficiently. It has increased our amount of usable data to over 80 percent and has cut down our project completion time to around six months in most cases."

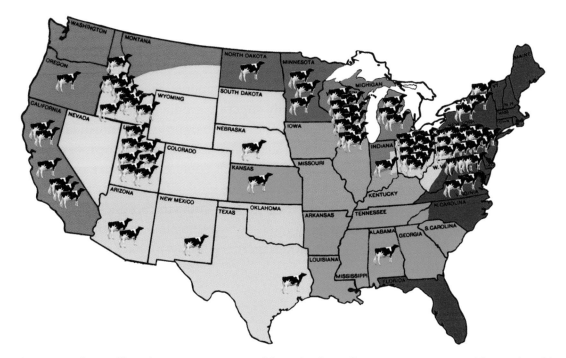

The Program for Fertility Advancement partners with 160 herds totaling 175,000 cows to provide a real-world environment for testing and proving the latest in Select Sires research.

PFA also helped to confirm the efficacy of two new semen extenders at Select Sires. DeJarnette mentions that a goal of the production department is to always look for better ways for sperm cells to survive freezing. In 2003, the cooperative was able to identify a new semen extender that was added to the existing egg yolk base for enhanced conception. Ensuing research allowed the production team to switch to a formula built around a milk-based extender. It has helped DeJarnette to fulfill his goal of "efficient utilization" meaning that lower performing bulls for fertility are enhanced because of the extender boost and higher fertility bulls can create more semen because we know the proper threshold for sperm cell counts in the semen.

Demand for additional semen from the membership and from around the world has also created a demand for more production facilities. Sales of 15 million units do not start and end with just producing 15 million units. As previously mentioned, some semen is immediately discarded for low quality and post-thaw quality measurement removes another seven to eight percent of semen from the inventory of saleable semen. Additional semen loss occurs from changing genetic information and shifting market demands. This means that to be able to sell 15 million doses of semen, production capabilities of closer to 18 million straws are required. Thus Select Sires has added people and remodeled facilities as the demand grew and dictated the need. A rough rule of thumb used in the production department is that a person is needed for every 500,000 straws produced and this has led to many additional people working in the department;

good people that are highly trained to understand the Select Sires way of producing semen.

The role of the board of directors, the farmer-owners that utilize Select Sires products and services, cannot be understated. With their support, the investments that are needed to deliver a highly fertile, genetically superior product have been made. The flow cytometer alone is a $100,000 investment in technology plus additional labor, that must be highly trained. It is an investment that offers a return in the form of a higher quality product. A company purely focused on profit could easily justify not making that investment. A cooperative structure provides the kind of feedback that determines the correct investments to make. Select Sires is the only company producing semen that uses a flow cytometer capable of making multiple assessments on semen at one time. The value in the flow cytometer is that motile sperm cells can still have damaged membranes and the machine catches that. The machine can also identify damaged DNA that interferes with normal embryogenesis impacting fertility; a microscope does not pick up this sensitive diagnosis.

Another investment that Select Sires innovated for the industry is gender-sorted semen. At the turn of the millennium it was becoming evident that the technology could exist for producing semen that had been sorted to deliver a majority of either male or female offspring and that the market would support such a product. There were a few companies that rushed to market with products that worked on paper but did not work in the field and that caused some doubt about whether the process could truly deliver a marketable product.

DeJarnette explains that the only method that really seemed to be working was a technology being developed by XY, Inc.: "In the late 1990s, we began the process of working with XY on the media needed for sorting sexed semen and the process that could be efficient enough for our membership. In the early 2000s, we finished a project in New York and the consensus was that the product wasn't quite ready for the marketplace. A few days later, a call from the marketing director at East Central/Select Sires came in and he mentioned that a sexed semen product was beginning to gain acceptance in Wisconsin. It turned out that this was the same product we had tested and we decided to rekindle the research."

The Select Sires board of directors encouraged the production department to continue researching the possibilities in the marketplace and a company headquartered in Texas, Sexing Technologies, was identified as a potential partner for producing a usable product. One of the owners, Juan Moreno, who had previously served as an intern at Select Sires, explained that his company had acquired the rights to a technology that was working with limited field testing. Select Sires had already established an efficient method of testing research in the field and became a logical partner as the first major A.I. company to exhaustively test the new technology on a larger scale. Select Sires sent five bulls to Texas. In early 2006, semen was sent to participating Select Sires customers to gauge the economics of the process for our members and the cooperative. The trial turned out just as expected, conception of the product showed a reduced fertility of approximately 20 to 25 percent but the product did deliver 90 percent of the desired gender, in this case heifer calves.

The membership encouraged Select Sires to continue with the process with one main request; improve the genetic level of the bulls available. With many of these high-ranking sires already in high demand, it was obvious that production days could not be lost by continually shipping sires to Texas. The decision was made to open a Sexing Technologies production facility in Ohio at the site of one of the former Select Embryo buildings and begin the large-scale production of gender SELECTed semen. Originally, four machines were installed but demand for the product with a good return on investment quickly increased the number of machines and collection schedules to where an excess of one million units could be produced annually. Gains in efficiency (initial technology processed 3,000 to 4,000 sperm cells per second while current digital technology can process 10,000 to 12,000 per second) have allowed the highest-ranking sires in the Select Sires lineup to be used in the program. With industry estimates projecting a growing percentage of semen sales to be of the gender-sorted variety, the gender SELECTed semen program at Select Sires remains an area of high focus and additional technologies continue to be researched.

Select Sires semen is sold to 95 countries around the world and producing a product that works the same in Kentucky as it does in China is a main area of focus. Continual domestic research coupled with market research abroad provides Select Sires with the feedback needed to be responsive to the needs of a growing customer base. Whether it is research that shows that the one-half cc straw is the preferred straw size by customers or innovations in extenders that keep the sperm cells healthier inside of the straw, the research team at Select Sires has constantly worked to deliver a better product to the customers of the cooperative. More than one million discarded units a year tell the story of a cooperative that is truly dedicated to fertility.

9

◆ ◆ ◆

Taking Solutions to the Farm

◆ ◆ ◆

"**I** was repro before repro was cool," says Dave Whitlock, reproductive specialist for Select Sire Power. He is referencing how the importance of providing reproductive help to the farm has gained in the period since the Select Reproductive Solutions (SRS) program formally began in 2006. That program will be looked at in more detail later, but Whitlock's channeling of an old Barbara Mandrell country song does reinforce the fact that until a program was formalized to take solutions to the farm, each member cooperative had their own methods for training and educating their members on the best methods for optimizing fertility in the herd. In many cases, member cooperatives did not even have people identified to focus on reproduction, in those cases the genetics person with the most interest in reproduction was recruited to chip in and troubleshoot problems or offer advice. It was a method that did not always succeed in helping the producer.

Just as the new millennium was beginning, a meeting of Select Sires personnel met in an oblong hotel room just outside of Chicago, Ill. The results of the meeting would change the direction of Select Sires forever and would chart the course for the best period of growth of the cooperative in Select Sires history. It was the transformation of Select Sires from a genetics company to a genetics and reproduction company.

Prior to the the Select Reproductive Solutions program formalizing the offering for member owners, individuals with an interest in reproductive consulting gathered to discuss what each member cooperative was doing to serve the customer.

In the closing years of the 20th century dairy farms around the world, and especially in the United States, were still predominantly traditional operations. The average herd size was 40 cows per herd in 1980 and by 2000 that number had grown to over 90. However the real telling figure is that in 1980, well over 25 percent of U.S. dairy cows were on farms with less than 75 cows and at the time of the meeting in Chicago, 25 percent of U.S. cows were on farms larger than 2,000 cows. The shift from individual cow-based-management to systems-based-herd management was well underway.

The discussion focused on the services and products that Select Sires needed to offer to remain the top choice of the American dairy producer and dairy cattle breeders around the world. The recurring theme of focus was that "it all started with a pregnancy." Select Sires had already earned the respect of breeders everywhere for delivering genetics that could help make their operations more profitable. Now, many producers realized the added profit sitting in their herds in the form of enhanced conception rates and pregnancy rates. These were terms that were not even in the lexicon of the typical Select Sires patron when the cooperative first began.

The meeting focused on the solutions that could be offered by Select Sires that would truly help the Select Sires customer-owners first understand the data and metrics that would help their herds, then establish programs and protocols that could be administered on the farm, and finally institute a method for measuring results and troubleshooting any issues that might arise. It was the birth of SRS.

Today, SRS is recognized as the world's leading program for analyzing and providing solutions to the needs of the progressive dairy farm. In just over 10 years, it has grown from a varied assortment of employees from different member cooperatives that may have been assigned the task because they had an interest in reproduction, to a team of dedicated professionals that focus solely on helping member-owners get their cattle pregnant at the rate that is optimum for their farm. It is ironic that this team's No. 1 goal is helping customers get cattle pregnant at a faster rate so less semen can be used. It seems contrary to the goals of a business that exists to sell as many units as possible but it is a goal that meets the charge of the mission statement perfectly:

To enhance the productivity and profitability of dairy and beef producers, Select Sires is committed to be the premier provider of highly fertile, superior genetics, accompanied by effective reproductive- and herd-management products and services.

A mission statement that has served Select Sires' customers well and an SRS program that has had tremendous leadership from the early days of reproductive solutions at Select Sires. One of these leaders is Ray Nebel, Ph.D.

Nebel grew up in southern Louisiana and quickly found respect as a top reproductive educator in stints at Louisiana State University, the USDA Beltsville Research Farm, North Carolina State University, and Virginia Tech. He was a popular speaker at dairy and beef events throughout the world and when he was hired, a fellow university researcher commented that, "A.I. companies have been after Ray for a lot of years, Select Sires was finally able to get it done." It was the availability of hands-on research coupled with the ability to still connect with the farmer that brought Nebel to Select Sires.

Dr. Ray Nebel has designed the Select Reproductive Solutions program to generate additional pregnancies for all sizes of farms in all environments.

It is no coincidence that Select Sires' leadership in helping to begin the Dairy Cattle Reproduction Council and sponsoring an on-site think tank for leading cattle reproduction researchers blossomed in the early years of the SRS program. Real solutions

Select Reproductive Solution specialists from across the country prepare to hone their techniques at Emerald Spring dairy.

need cutting-edge research. Cutting-edge research comes from the latest developments in timed A.I., activity systems, technician training and the other services that occur on the farm. Bringing experts together to share notes has led to many new programs and products that benefit the dairy and cattle managers of the new millennium. The 1996 "Estrus Synchronization Brainstorming Session" that started with seven university researchers has grown to an annual "think tank" incorporating as many as 70 researchers from university and allied industry. Mel DeJarnette, vice president of research and quality control at Select Sires, mentions that "getting all of these people together to discuss and share unpublished data doesn't always give us the answers, but it does always lead us to better questions."

Timed-A.I., activity systems and formalized technician training like we have today did not exist in 1965. The basic skills of simple artificial insemination existed but there wasn't much else to separate basic reproductive results from outstanding reproductive results. Thus, genetics were the difference maker when a customer compared their options in selecting sires for their breeding program. Changes in management styles and cattle environments meant that new tools and resources needed to be developed to assist the modern dairy and beef cattle producers in getting their cattle safe with calf. There were so many new tools and options that the average producers needed assistance to stay ahead of the growing challenges their breeding programs were experiencing. The goal of the early days of SRS was to simplify the system and methods for getting cattle pregnant so that the customer could focus on genetics again.

This book will not focus on the history of timed-A.I. and other synchronization protocols that ushered in the need for reproductive management, but will take a review of how SRS was able to take national pregnancy rates that hovered around 15 percent at the inception of the program to national pregnancy rates of more than 20 percent today with many herds achieving 30 percent pregnancy rates and better.

One of the advantages of the Select Sires business model and service coverage area has always been the geography covered by the members of the federation. Whereas a privately owned company might solely base their decision on the potential profit of a decision to offer service in an area, Select Sires and the federation of cooperatives that form it made decisions with farmer-based boards giving direction. This meant that the ability to make a profit was still part of the consideration but not until all alternatives and variables impacting the decision were considered. Considerations such as the potential for industry growth in the area and the ability to provide service at a breakeven cost even if it did not have a certain profit margin allowed Select Sires to provide services that other companies did not.

So when it came time to implement SRS to the masses, Joel Mergler, vice president of training and animal health products, recommended a "train the trainer" concept to take the program to as many farms and cooperatives as possible. This concept allowed the highest level of specialist within the Select Sires federation to touch as many customers as possible through other highly trained specialists at the individual member cooperative level. Two-thirds of most reproductive troubleshooting can be done at the member level with individual SRS specialists at each cooperative. When a situation arises that needs a little extra review, the local specialist can gather the data and pass it along to a specialist with additional training and expertise. It is again an example of the cooperative way and the focus on sharing resources that remains a hallmark of Select Sires.

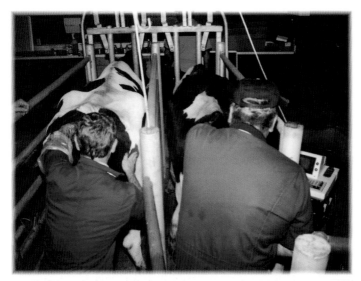

Select Check training offers employees an education on skills that benefit the modern dairy such as synch protocols, pregnancy awareness, and ultrasound techniques.

The roster of SRS specialists is a diverse group. The group consists of technicians, Select Mating Service (SMS) evaluators, area sales managers and individuals whose sole focus is reproductive solutions. Whatever the career and whatever the background, the interest in learning and additional education must be present for the SRS specialist to remain in the program. It is the dedication to training and continuing education that

The Select Reproductive Solutions conference offers reproductive specialists the opportunity to share ideas and learn the latest developments for generating pregnancies on the farm.

makes the difference for a Select Sires SRS specialist.

An example of this is Julie Ainsworth. She became the Dairy Production Analysis and Select Reproduction Coordinator at NorthStar Cooperative but she began as a dairy mating evaluator. She explains, "I originally started with dairy production analysis in 1993. I wanted a way to explain why the matings would not appear to be working in a particular herd. In those days facility design was often the culprit. I really started the reproductive focus when we started the SRS program with Ray. Over time I have learned to present strengths and opportunities in a clear concise manner without overloading the producer with information. I have also learned to cater my recommendations to the individual producer since everyone has their own learning style."

This additional learning takes place in the form of SRS conferences that have been held annually since 2005. The conferences are successful because they bring the SRS team members together to exchange ideas, share trends that they are seeing in the marketplace and even compete on reproductive analysis abilities. The internal discussions are complemented with the inclusion of outside speakers covering the latest research on synchronization protocols, activity systems, nutrition, pharmaceuticals and health products. At the conclusion of the week, follow-up information and learning exercises are placed on Select Sires' in-house education site, the Center for Excellence. The same site also serves as a treasure trove of reproductive educational materials and industry articles that supplement the learning. From the latest synchronization research to the newest cattle monitoring software, the SRS specialist has instant access to the tools and handouts that can make an improvement in reproductive results for today's beef and dairy cattle manager.

SRS utilizes three key components to implement these tools at the producer level and to gauge the progress that has been made on the farm. These components are the Select RePRO Analysis™ program, SelectCheck™ reproductive skills training and the method for generating (SelectSynch and timed-A.I.) or recognizing cattle in estrus (activity aystems).

Select RePRO Analysis is probably the most recognizable component of the SRS program. Developed by Virginia dairy producer Tom Alexander, this analysis program pulls data from all major herd management software programs to sort, separate, and analyze the reproductive performance of the herd. Key performance indicators such as days in milk at time of conception, performance by lactation group, conception rates by time of breeding and countless other measures are pulled together in handy reports and graphs for use in the reproductive management of the farm. Continuing to update the reports on a timely basis allows the herd manager to track performance over time and to implement changes and new standard operating procedures that will benefit the reproductive performance of the herd.

Julie Ainsworth, Dairy Production Analysis and Reproduction Services Coordinator at Northstar Cooperative visits with customer Aaron Gasper about his results.

Dave Whitlock credits this part of the program as one of the biggest advantages to having a formalized, focused system for analyzing herds. "When I first started in this position, we focused on the technicians and the semen quality. Today, we know that it takes a lot more than a technician to generate a pregnancy. We have learned how import-

Imported	1733	Pregnant
Cows	950	436
Heifers	783	248

Last Data Entry 9/24/14
Voluntary Waiting Period (VWP) 61

Item	SRS Benchmarks National	Regional	Current Status	Herd Benchmarks
% Preg > VWP		50	61	
% Preg > VWP < 150 DIM			46	
% Confirmed Preg 3 Cycles Past VWP			40	
% Confirmed Preg for Desired Calving Interval[1]			47	
Days in Milk at First Service (DIMFS)	~90	80	73	
% DIMFS > 100 DIM	~30	20	0	
% Open > 270 DIM		1	9	
% DNB	~6	5	6	
% Heat Detection Rate	~50	60	67	
% Conception Rate First Service	~38	40	37	
% Conception Rate All Services	~35	35	31	
% Average 21-day Pregnancy Rate	~16	20	22	
% Heat Detection Rate, Last 120 days	~50	60	71	
% Conception First Service, Last 120 days	~38	40	39	
% Conception Rate, All Services, Last 120 days	~35	35	36	
% Conception Rate, Lac = 1, Last 120 days	~35	35	38	
% Conception Rate, Lac > 1, Last 120 days	~35	35	30	
% Average 21-day Pregnancy Rate, Last 120 days	~16	20	21	
Average Days in Milk		160	176	
Average Days Open		150	125	
Current Test Day Milk (lb)		67	82	
Current Somatic Cell Count (1000)	~250	250	2	
% Cows < 250000 SCC	~50	80	100	

RePRO Analysis software helps to identify bottlenecks on the farm and assists the SRS specialist in identifying recommendations for improvement.

ant transition cow management is to reproduction, along with synchronization, cow comfort, udder health, early pregnancy detection and a host of other factors. Select RePRO Analysis allows me to have a lot more detail, be a lot more professional, and to take a more holistic approach to helping the producer."

SelectCheck, along with other employee training, ensures that a Select Sires employee providing service to a member's farm has the skills necessary to help the farm and move them to a higher level of performance. One to two weeks of offsite-training is held at a participating large herd facility and provides education in skills that are needed by the modern Select Sires employee to be a key member of today's professional dairy or beef operation. Training in synchronization protocols, reproductive physiology, pregnancy awareness, data analysis and other service skills that Select Sires provides to the customer gives an intensive course in optimizing pregnancies generated on the farm. Ray Nebel, King Smith and Earl Ingram form the team that develop and run the SelectCheck training. As a native Spanish speaker, Ingram serves as an important connection between Select Sires and the growing number of Latino employees on the modern US dairy farm.

The final key component of the program is identifying the best tools available to the farm for producing animals to be inseminated. Today a cattle owner has many tools available but it still comes down to two main techniques, identifying an animal in estrus or synchronizing the ovulation of the animal. In 1965, the main tool for identifying an animal in estrus was a visual observation of the cow followed by the a.m./p.m. rule to inseminate her approximately 12 hours later. Technology can now be employed to make these visual observations by measuring the activity of the animal and comparing that activity to the baseline of the herd. Additional technology, such as rumination monitoring, make the measurements even more accurate and provides additional data for monitoring and affecting the performance of the herd. Synchronization of ovulation does away with the need for the observation of estrus and activity. A herd can use reproductive hormones to time ovulation, eliminating the need for additional heat detection or labor. An SRS specialist is trained in the options available to the herd and can give advice on the best reproductive decision considering the management and economics of the individual farm.

It should come as no surprise that many of the SRS specialists in the program today have a strong connection to technician work for the cooperative. Adam Hahlen began as a technician for COBA/Select Sires in 1986 after earning an associate's degree from Ohio State University Agricultural Technical Institute. While working as a technician, Hahlen completed his bachelor's degree in marketing and moved into a role that provided reproductive troubleshooting in 1994. In 2002, he added the duties of technician coordinator before becoming a full-fledged SRS reproductive specialist when the program formally started in 2006. The transition has been a natural one as Select Sires technicians have the closest connection to the customer of anyone in the cooperative. Hahlen's connection to the technician team helps strengthen that connection to the customer as he states, "I go to work every day to help my customers succeed. The service we provide our customer-owners is free. We independently look at their herd's success and evaluate their areas of weakness and strength. While each customer has a different breeding pattern, all of our customers have the same end goal – to produce an efficient pregnancy. SRS can help achieve that."

IBM was once just a company that made computers but their success really took off when they began to offer services that could best capitalize on their core business of making computers. In many ways the SRS program is Select Sires' version of that transition to services that go along with our core product of genetics. Breeders have always looked to Select Sires for the best seedstock genetics available. The ability to have better results when using those genetics with SRS was a game changer that elevated Select Sires to become the trusted partner in the success of operations around the world. If you are going to build anything that goes upward, any experienced builder will tell you that a strong base is crucial for support. The genetics were the first element of the base and the SRS program is additional framework that expands the foundation for the customers of Select Sires to reach new heights.

♦ ♦ ♦

The Genomic Era

♦ ♦ ♦

The Greek philosopher Heraclitus is known for coining the phrase, "You could not step twice into the same river." It was his way of saying that things are always changing and even though something might look the same, there is a strong possibility that the situation is fundamentally different. An original concentration on traits may give way to newly discovered traits or traits that can now be tracked with the assistance of technology. Perhaps the discovery that had the biggest impact on genetic selection was the introduction of genomic analysis to the process. Some industry observers would say it took the babbling brook of breeding and genetic selection and turned it into a raging river of DNA and accelerated generations. In any case, the selection of sires for use in a modern breeding program will "never step in the same river again."

A statement in the April 24, 2009 report in the journal Science that the three billion base pairs of the bovine genome had been sequenced foreshadowed the potential that the discovery might have when it said that the results are "likely to have a major impact on livestock breeding." For the first time, researchers and sire analysts alike could have access to the genomic profile of an animal to make breeding decisions and marketing decisions as soon as DNA was present to be inspected.

Dave Thorbahn, Jeff Ziegler, Shirley Kaltenbach and Chris England and members of the Board of Directors visit with one of the first offspring resulting from the Aggressive Reproductive Technologies (ART) program.

Previously, a young sire sampling schedule would identify a female that was at least two years old and analyze her for conformation and production performance. Then that animal would be contracted for a male offspring that would arrive in nine months if everything went well. That animal would be tested and brought into stud for young sire sampling that would begin after the animal had reached one year of age, most likely in the 14 to16 month age bracket. That semen would be used in cooperator herds and calves would result nine months later. The heifers would be raised as replacements on the farm and two years later we would have an animal that could be analyzed for conformation and production performance. All totaled, the process from creating the bull calf to the ability to say the creation was a successful result took five years.

Fast-forward to the genomic era and one will notice that the process has been accelerated quite a bit. A calf with any DNA (hair, blood, tissue swab, etc.) can be analyzed for the genomic DNA information present. At a very young age, we have a profile that has been matched to profiles of thousands of other animals telling us the projection for conformation, production performance and health traits. The most outstanding profiles are selected for mating to that of the opposite sex. As mentioned in the previous chapter, Select Sires wants to validate and confirm all matings through sampling in the PGA young sire program. However, the technology is advanced enough that if a genomic profile is exceptional, that animal will enter the program to create future sires before the animal has offspring on the ground. Hundreds of thousands of previously tested animals combined with new technology analyzing the data gives confidence to the results of the modern genomic animal. Multiple research projects analyzing genomics against performance shows that there can still be an occasional outlier that moves more than expected, but as a group the performance of genomic predicted offspring is very consistent with expectations. Select Sires' own research shows that a sire very seldom moves more than a quartile in either direction. A bull in the top quartile at the time of sampling will assuredly be in the top half of sires when additional performance data is included. Increases in reliability of genomic data means that selecting sires for entry into the Select Sires program must be carefully planned. If a sire analyst previously spent 70 percent of their time looking at cattle in the field, he or she may well now spend that same amount of time with a computer screen looking at the results and potential results of different genomic combinations.

It also causes a cooperative serving member-owners to take steps to ensure that the best genetics available today are utilized in a sire sampling program. Traditionally, the way to acquire a sire was to identify a female with desirable genes, mate that female to a male with desirable complementary genes, and then sample the genes of the resulting offspring across the population of cattle to gauge performance.

Today, that method is still being utilized, but the leadership of Select Sires directed the sire department to take additional steps on a new program that will accelerate genetic progress and also lend greater control of desirable genes in the cattle breeding industry. The program is directed to provide more rapid generation intervals while also creating sires that meet the needs of member-owners of the cooperative that otherwise might not be met by popular breeding strategies. That program is the Aggressive Reproductive Technology (ART) program and it attempts to keep the art of breeding great cattle alive and well at Select Sires.

The ART program exists for the main purpose of creating sires that meet the needs of the modern dairy cattle breeder. No two dairy cattle owners are alike and each breeder has a slightly different set of breeding goals when they select a sire for use in their mating program. Jeff Ziegler, the first manager of the ART program said, "We felt compelled to broaden our range of bloodlines to give dairy producers more options when making genetic selections. We wanted to create additional genetic variation and also utilize genomic tools to slow the inbreeding growth of the Holstein breed."

When the program first began, sires such as 7HO9545 HERO, 7HO9173 PLATO, 7HO9052 MORPHEOUS and 7HO9030 RICHMAN were not in wide use as sire fathers but did sire offspring for use in the ART program. The sires mentioned might not have had an overall profile that had widespread demand for genetic seedstock selection but each of the sires did provide traits that will benefit certain segments of the industry and fit a need for current niche breeding that can often become a more widely demanded trait.

Part of the team that manages the Select Sires Calf Campus observe some of the new arrivals shortly after the campus opened in 2011. L-R: Brett Kneeskern, Adam Oswalt, Sarah Groce and Janeen Hartman.

ART also began the process of Select Sires purchasing females for use in the program. In 2009, the Select Sires board of directors, consisting of farmers from coast to coast, directed management to find new and improved ways of securing sires for use by the membership. Through this instruction, the ART program was created and approval was given for female acquisition. Elite females were purchased with plans to purposely breed them to create sires with a desirable breeding pattern for Select Sires customers. Along with the purchase of females, approval was granted to purchase embryos for the program. This allowed the ART program to get a head start on the genomic profiles that were in demand. The genomic giant 7HO11314 MOGUL entered the ART program as a purchased embryo and quickly lent credibility to the power of genomics. In the same irony that goes along with 7HO8081 PLANET, part of the allure of MOGUL was the fact that his pedigree was considered an "outcross" to the popular pedigrees of the day. His tremendous performance ensures that he will be a sire that gets mentioned in the pedigrees of "No MOGUL" outcross sires of the future.

It was a bold move by the board to approve female acquisition and embryo purchases. They were focused on doing the right thing for the most customer-owners, as the board realized that some individual breeders might view the concept as an infringement on their marketing plans. Fortunately, the grassroots direction that comes from the member cooperatives supported the decision and most of the objection was localized and short-lived. It allowed the program to introduce some unique pedigrees and breeding methods to Select Sires from a maternal side.

Even with the desire to utilize the females for high-ranking offspring, the females purchased and developed by Select Sires are still expected to perform in milking form. ART cooperator herds are located around the country and these herds house the females after an in vitro fertilization (IVF) program is completed. The well-managed, commercial-style dairies calve in the animals, they are classified and their performance is analyzed just like any other bull dam. It is another step in assuring that the genetics available to the customer-owners of Select Sires perform as expected at the farm level where they are being used, and also assuring that no special treatment is given that might affect the data.

"As herds require different mating approaches to fit within their management programs, ART will have to be customized to fit their needs," Ziegler adds. Owning a few females allows Select Sires to quickly adapt to these new, cost-effective methods of building the very best set of sampling sires in the industry." The expectation is that the ART program will produce about 30 percent of the sires that enter the Select Sires lineup. Animals produced for the program carry the "S-S-I" prefix and enter the PGA progeny test program just like any other sire. It is not a cheap process, but it is a necessary investment by Select Sires to ensure that the members of the federation always have access to top genetics that meet their needs.

Another consideration of the investment that Select Sires has made in bull acquisition is the importance of having rights to first choice in a flush for a contract mating. Sire selection was assisted by visual observation at the farm in the pre-genomic era. The sire analyst went to the farm and used physical conformation and scrotal circumference to make the selection decision because full brothers from the flush of a like sire and dam would all have the same parent average. In some cases, those young bulls would have a very similar physical makeup and the premium between having the first choice or the fourth choice would be negligible. Genomic data changed all of that. A report might signify a few hundred TPI points of extra performance on a first choice compared to lower ranking choices. Having the first option during acquisition is a crucial part of acquiring bulls for the program. If there is a recurring theme to Select Sires, it is having good people work for the cooperative that have the relationships with good people on the farm. The sire analysts' relationship with the breeders is just one more example of this, providing our customer-owners with the best sires.

Following the research that developed the ART program, the StrataGEN program was created to help producers make simplified breeding decisions. It was recognized as one of Dairy Herd Management magazine's Top Innovations for 2012. Complete information about how the StrataGEN program functions is addressed in the chapter on Select Mating Service (SMS), but it is genomic information that powered the technology behind this innovative line breeding program. Research on inbreeding from Bennett Cassell, Ph.D., shows that for every 1 percent of inbreeding increase, performance is impacted by a decrease of 790 pounds of milk and a decrease of 24 Net Merit dollars among other undesirable effects. Placing sires into one of five specific breeding lines allows for a significant reduction in inbreeding across lines. A traditional pedigree analysis would allow sires to be placed in a line based on their parent average and pedigree. The power of genomic testing greatly increased the knowledge of which genetics are present and in which line a sire should be placed. It is just another example of how genomic research and testing has given the industry additional tools to make breeding decisions. The StrataGEN program, which is called the SelectaGEN program in Canada, has increased genetic gain on farms while delivering on the promise of a simple, time saving program for ease of use.

From the beginning, dairy producers wanted programs that would provide a positive return and were based on sound research. It was for these reasons, dairy producers trusted the sires and services of Select Sires. An outsider could look at dairy cattle breeding and come to the conclusion that there is nothing new that could happen in a mature industry that has been around since the beginning of mechanized agriculture. New innovations do come along and cattle breeders need to have the ability to rely on a company that they can trust to make the right decisions. Genomics offered an opportunity to Select Sires when other competitors in the industry saw it as a threat. Planning, research and action allowed Select Sires to offer the member-owners of the cooperative multiple options for utilizing genomics. Through innovative programs like ART and StrataGEN, the Select Sires customer could capitalize on the new tool of genomics without a lot of personal investment. It is another example of the cooperative way.

Retiring General Manager Dick Chichester congratulates David Thorbahn on his appointment as the 4th General Manager in Select Sires history.

◆ ◆ ◆

An Interview with David Thorbahn

◆ ◆ ◆

When longtime General Manager Dick Chichester announced his retirement in 1999, the Board of Directors of Select Sires initiated a nationwide search for the next leader of the cooperative. With many qualified applicants, the board wanted to ensure that their selection could guide the company to achieve the goals of the membership. At the time, the Board President was Charles Moellendick and he reviewed the process as such, "…after the interviews we went around the table and got feedback from the committee. It was clear that Dave had the vision for Select Sires that would serve us well and the drive to get the plan executed." Thus, David Thorbahn was named the next leader of Select Sires and he took the helm on January 1, 2000.

Our interview occurred in the spring of 2014. Spring is a time of renewal, at the time of the interview the grass was turning green and the trees were starting to blossom in Ohio. It was a fitting time to revisit some of the new programs and products that occurred at Select Sires under Dave's leadership.

What led to your interest in the genetics and reproduction industry?

Thorbahn: I grew up on a family dairy farm with registered cattle. We had 130 cows plus young stock and farmed 600 acres two hours north of Plain City, Ohio.

What was your school and work experience before coming to Select Sires?

Thorbahn: My enjoyment was always the cows and my plan was always to go and farm with my dad. With two older brothers and one great uncle on the farm, there was no room for me so I went to Ohio State and majored in dairy science with a strong genetic focus. After schooling I went to another A.I. company working 15 years there with 12 years as a sire analyst and later as the manager of their sire development program. I was working in Wisconsin and I took two years while working to get my master of business administration degree from the University of Wisconsin at Madison. Around that time it was announced that Dick Chichester was retiring and Select Sires would be looking for a new general manager. A couple of friends that knew my interests encouraged me to apply. I was sure I had no chance but I had strong interest and did apply. Being an "outsider" I am confident that I had little support going into the interview. Fortunately during the process with the board, we realized that my goals and their goals meshed and I was selected at the interview as the next leader of Select Sires. I began with Select Sires on August 31, 1999 in order to spend some time learning under Mr. Chichester.

What are some of your memories of your beginnings at Select Sires?

Thorbahn: The very first assignment that Dick gave me was to return a call to DuWayne Kutz. DuWayne was the manager of Sire Power and they had interest in joining Select Sires. This led to us sitting down with the three boards that would be involved; Select Sires, Sire Power and Virginia-North Carolina. We discussed the proper way to put that together, which was putting Sire Power's membership area together with Virginia-North Carolina's membership area that was very congruent. This provided return in two main ways. The first way was that the Sire Power membership could benefit by getting access to bulls and programs that they otherwise did not have. DuWayne was a forward thinker and saw the value they could provide to the Sire Power membership. Select Sires benefitted because it allowed us to go from 215 Holstein bulls to 300 Holstein bulls being sampled a year. This was the engine that gave us the major growth that we achieved from 2000 to 2013 allowing us to accomplish our goal of doubling the size of the company. DuWayne Kutz's foresight and commitment to his breeders was the catalyst that allowed this to become reality.

The next big thing was something that I noticed at my former employer; that

Select Sires had the best bulls for production and type but struggled in Canada. Sales were at 50,000 units annually and we knew the potential was there for the Canadian market. We took the model for the member organization that has worked so well domestically and patterned Select Sires Canada after that model. This has worked and has allowed us to grow from 2 percent market share in Canada to 13 percent market share and selling 250,000

Dave Thorbahn, DuWayne Kutz, and Wayne Dudley, the General Manager's of Select Sires, Sire Power, and VA/NC Select Sires respectively join in a toast to the new entity of Select Sire Power.

units a year (as of 2013 data). The reality is that the passion that Select Sires customers have in breeding truly great cattle is the same for Canadian breeders. Our manager in Canada, Bill Young, has built the business there the same way our member organizations have done it and that is to have great people. That is the reality of Select Sires, the people make the organization great. The other thing that Canada allowed us to do is to source genetics and progeny test 25 bulls in Canada beginning in March 2000. Today Select Sires GenerVations is paying Program for Genetic Advancement Canada™ (PGAC™) credits to those participating producers.

The third big step was with our international marketing. Bill Clark, the owner of World Wide Sires, was ready to sell his business. World Wide Sires marketed Select Sires semen to the eastern hemisphere of the world and was a key part of our global success. We knew we wanted to stay involved but we did not have enough semen to meet the global demand. Select Sires' philosophy has always been to allocate production to domestic markets first where our member-owners reside. So we needed a partner to make the World Wide Sires transaction work and that partner ended up being Accelerated Genetics. CRI had already pulled out of World Wide Sires and this was the natural fit. Together we completed the purchase July 1, 2001 and World Wide Sires, LTD was born. The organization was set up to first pay back the original investment of both owners and then would be a "pass through" organization that benefitted the organization that sold the semen rather than be an organization that generates large profits for World Wide Sires. Again, great people like John Schouten and the entire sales and order fulfillment team came along with World Wide Sires. Bill Clark had a great staff and that has benefitted all organizations. World Wide Sires quickly recovered from what could have been a big blow in losing CRI and has generated tremendous growth for Select Sires sales across the globe. These sales also benefit member-owners as they use up excess inventory and provided cash for new investment.

Those three factors prepared us for a major period of growth and we have seen consistent benefits from those moves all along.

What internal moves have benefitted Select Sires?

Thorbahn: In 2001, the Select Sires board and members of Select Sires staff got together and the board led a process of strategic planning that led to one of the strongest growth periods in our organization's history. This process allowed us to focus on each of the areas of our company that touch our customers. One was in serving the members and another was in harvesting sperm cells in a high quality manner.

Clif Marshall and Mel DeJarnette led a great revolution of innovation that increased the quantity and quality of our semen to meet demands of growing markets. By using new techniques and capitalizing on research we were able to double the productivity of our bulls while increasing fertility at the same time. We knew that some bulls appeared to perform better with a varied production schedule so we really went to whatever collection schedule the bull preferred. Dr. Don Monke, Clif and Mel really worked with the schedules to fine tune them for optimum sperm cell production. It took a lot of dedication from the production team to find the optimum collection schedule for each bull.

Even more important than the quantity increase was the increase in fertility that our customer-owners experienced during this time. The board of directors had always had a sire committee to give member input on the type of genetics our company should acquire for the membership. They decided that a fertility oversight committee would be equally as productive to ensure that everything that Select Sires does with fertility is for the benefit of the dairy and beef producer. The board wanted to be assured that Select Sires was aggressive in research to improve fertility, while making sure that all changes in processing were for the betterment of the customer-owner. The first committee (Production Review Committee) included Johnny Daniel, who has a master's degree in reproductive physiology, Dr. Bob Cruikshank, DVM, and Dr. Mark Tatarka, DVM. All were highly trained individuals who also happened to have productive farms and serve on our board. The input from that committee and the board set in motion the major investments in flow cytometry, processing systems and research that Select Sires put into the Program for Fertility Advancement.

What were some of the other memorable moves forward for the cooperative?

Thorbahn: Our next revolution was the hiring of Dr. Ray Nebel to our team. Ray was always respected as the foremost reproductive physiologist in the United States in the field of heat detection and female reproductive physiology as it relates to synchronization. A lot of researchers were working with synch protocols, but Ray could best put it together with what we knew about estrus detection and cycles. This was our biggest move beyond being just a genetics company. Up to that point we had been a genetics company, now we could be passionate about reproduction also. It led to the start of our Select Reproductive Solutions (SRS) program to take results to the membership. We started in 2007 with five SRS specialists that solely focused on repro to now employing more than 50 people whose main directive is assisting our members to get better results with reproduction.

Along with that, Ray developed the Select RePRO Analysis program that provided a tool for our SRS specialists to use to analyze on-farm records and make recommendations to the customer on reproductive efficiency. Ray worked with a member of the cooperative who has a dairy in Virginia, Tom Alexander, to develop this program. Again we have a case of a member of the cooperative chipping in with talents and skills to help move the entire cooperative forward.

What are some of the most recent developments at Select Sires?

Thorbahn: Well, by 2007 we felt that we had all the pistons in place to really fuel growth and meet demand for the Select Sires products and services. That usually is a good time to start again on strategic planning and the needs of the cooperative going forward, so that is what we did. In 2008, the board again had a major strategic planning session to identify the needs of our membership going forward.

The first item that was identified was a concern about pharmaceutical availability going forward. The U.S. dairy industry had a watershed moment where an approved item for on-farm use was getting crushed in the marketplace (Posilac). There was no telling which item might be next to come under the crosshairs and the board knew that we better start preparations for what Select Sires could offer the membership if certain tools were to be removed from the reproductive solutions toolbox. It was obvious that we needed to bring in some new technology that could very accurately predict the activity of an animal indicating her estrus levels. The Select Detect^{TM} system proved to be a very effective tool in doing that. Later, with a need

David Thorbahn with the 10 member managers shortly after taking the job in 2001. Back L-R: Herald Catlin, Tim Riley, David Thorbahn, Wayne Dudley, Lyle Kruse and Ferron Perkes. Front L-R: Bernie Heisner, Mike Goggin, Al Deming, Mike Bills and Paul Kunkel.

*for some rumination monitoring as well, we also began to handle the SCR Heatime®
system. Both activity systems had proven to be very effective. Today, Agis CowManager is the newest generation of repro, rumination and feeding management – all
through an ear tag.*

*The second phase covered in our strategic planning was how to address the increase in feed costs that many dairy and beef producers were facing. As a result,
Select Sires Vice President of Genetic Programs, Chuck Sattler, initiated research in
feed efficiency and eventually identified traits and genetics that can do a good job of
predicting overall efficiency in a proprietary formula. This is how our FeedPRO index came to be and we also added a few other selection indexes taking into account
the need of commercial producers for moderately sized cattle. It simplifies selection
criteria for our members that prefer to systematically select the sires that they use
on their farms.*

*Finally, there was an increasing concern about inbreeding in the industry. Mating
programs have always done a great job of managing inbreeding but the manage-*

ment styles of some farms do not allow them to utilize Select Mating Service. Thus we developed two programs, Aggressive Reproductive Technologies™ (ART™) and StrataGEN that helped to simplify the use of our sires to gain production and health traits while avoiding inbreeding. The ART program allows us to put genetics together in our sires that the seed stock supplier of our bulls might not want to otherwise provide. The StrataGEN program is specifically designed to control inbreeding because lines of genetics are formed allowing each individual line to be highly related genetically but then very different from the other genetics in the population. Following a rotation of lines allows breeders utilizing the StrataGEN program to have very low inbreeding coefficients.

One other move that was made around this same time was reducing the size of the board of directors. Our board had grown to a size considered larger than was needed because of mergers and other acquisitions. At this time, we reduced the board to our current size of 18 members. This allows a leaner, more cohesive group to take action and hold productive discussion on the best course for the future of Select Sires.

With all of the growth in sales, what has Select Sires done to keep up with production?

Thorbahn: In 2008 to 2009, we outgrew our production capabilities and it was obvious we had to do some building. In 2009, we renovated the Hecker Center and that gave us 28 additional production stalls. In 2010, we built our two new European Union (EU) barns that gave us 88 additional stalls. In 2011, we increased the expansion of our admittance facilities at Darby Creek to house young stock less than eight months of age. Building that facility was primarily to receive these extreme ART bulls and give them the highest level of healthcare possible. A fringe benefit of those new barns was that we could bring in other sires earlier as well and we saw an increase in the health of the animals as well as an increase in scrotal circumference. That doesn't sound like much but it makes a big difference in the ability to produce additional volumes of semen at an earlier age.

Can you explain the reason for recent success of Select Sires in more detail?

Thorbahn: The recent success starts with the leadership of the board of directors. Select Sires has been blessed with strong leadership from the board of directors with consecutive talented presidents and board members who are committed to making Select Sires all it can be. The 2008 board of director's strategic planning session was a strong example where the board challenged management to research solutions to reduce inbreeding, identify feed efficient cattle, and find effective tools to identify natural occurring heats. From this challenge, Select Sires employees focused on possible solutions to resolve issues for today's dairy and beef producers. From that, ART, StrataGEN, FeedPRO and innovative heat detection devices were researched. These programs allowed the Select Sires federation to raise the level of service to farmer-owners to new heights. The board also gave employees unwavering support and financing to aggressively embrace the new genomic tools in both traditional selection as well as the investment into Aggressive Reproductive Technologies (ART) to enhance our genetic offering for our customers. This was the catalyst to allow dedicated employees the tools they needed to grow our business.

Dedicated people also include the employees back at the member organizations. To serve a greater share of customers, we need additional technicians, sales representatives, support personnel (such as SRS and SMS specialists) and coordination with Select Sires to collect, ship and distribute the product that they need. The growth from six million units to 14 million units sold annually that we have seen in the past 15 years all comes back to those passionate and talented people. We would have never seen the stability that we had during that time while other competitors were struggling without those talented people. In 2009, the dairy industry saw one of the most difficult economic environments in history. The board of directors and member managers made a commitment to our people during that time that we would not lay people off, we would not change commissions and we would not change benefits at a time when this was common in the industry. What this meant was that a lot of other industry professionals looked at how Select Sires treated its people and joined Select Sires during this time.

This demonstrates the culture that Select Sires ownership has throughout the organization. From the board to the managers to the employees, our growth is because our organization recognizes the value of people. Training people properly and treating them with respect is a key to our success. Then all we have to do is keep people focused in the right direction and the customer-owner will reward us with their business.

What do you see in the future for Select Sires?

Thorbahn: Future tools for dairymen and cattle owners are tools that include the value of data. So, we have to focus on new tools including sexed semen, improved semen quality, improved semen fertility and use those tools to deliver an animal that has more value. Specifically, targeting the proper breed and the right type of cow that is totally focused on the people who are consuming dairy and beef products from our customers. The genetics company that can engineer innovations and solutions for customers to meet the needs of their customers will continue to be winners in the industry. The future of animal agriculture is bright because we will have to double food production for a growing population with only a five to seven percent growth in arable land. The excitement comes from getting that growth through technology and genetics to improve productivity so that we can feed the world with high-quality protein.

To do this, we will continue to unlock our understanding of genetics. We are really only beginning to understand why genetics are turned on and off. For Select Sires to remain as a major factor in feeding the world, we will need to do research and ensure that these technologies are controlled by many rather than one. Competition will allow us to improve our ability to serve the customer that owns Select Sires. Bernie Heisner, retired general manager of COBA/Select Sires, gave me a great example that supports this. "In 1980, a bag of seed corn cost $60 and a unit of semen was generally around $25. Today, a bag of seed corn costs $250 to $300 and a unit of semen generally sells for around $20." Now the second part of that comparison is productivity. In 1980 our top Ohio herds had a 16,000 pound herd average and we could get 112 bushels per acre of corn. Today we are at a 28,000 to 30,000 pound herd average and we get 180 bushels per acre of corn. There are differences involved in each but the return on investment is affected by who owns the product.

So that brings us to the Council on Dairy Cattle Breeding. It is important for the data farmers provide to remain farmer-owned and controlled. The majority of the member organizations of the council are all farmer-owned; the DHI centers are farmer-owned, the breed associations are farmer-owned, and most of the NAAB members are farmer-owned like cooperatives Select Sires, Accelerated Genetics, and CRI. To ensure equal representation and fairness in investments, innovations that benefit producers must remain farmer-owned and controlled.

Any final thoughts on the 50-year success of Select Sires?

Thorbahn: As we look to the future, we must copy the success manual of the past: which is to hire, train, and motivate great people. Select Sires history is filled with committed, honorable and hardworking leaders in every division of its company that have elevated the industry in some way. I have been fortunate to work with many of those.

Shirley Kaltenbach, Select Sires director of communications, authored the brand promise "Your Success Our Passion" that describes this very well. This promise embraces the rich agricultural heritage of employees throughout the Select Sires federation. This promise resonates with the deep rich talent within the federation and elicits the heritage of many employees which give them their love for the cattle industry and the cattle owners. Kaltenbach and her talented team have embraced this history in this promise and in their communication efforts as a reminder for us to carry this heritage forward.

In addition to the communications team, I have also been fortunate to work with Dr. Don Monke, V.P. of Production Operations, and his team who have made great contributions to industry in biosecurity and quality bull care to allow bulls to make high quality semen. The processing and quality control, led by Clif Marshall and his team have made Select Sires semen quality the envy of the industry. Mel DeJarnette has been given the charge of leading into the next chapter of product quality. I have had the honor and privilege of working with Ron Long and then Charles Sattler and their teams, who have kept genetics at the corner stone of Select Sires which has impacted the entire industry through its great sires. Roy Wallace, Brian House, Aaron Arnett and Luke Bowman have made Select Sires the stud you can rely on for beef sires that produce the highest quality carcasses. Chris England has led the finance, human resources and information systems teams that have kept Select Sires sound, well financed, and operating smoothly. In addition, our talented marketing team of professionals, Blaine Crosser, Lyle Kruse, Joel Mergler, Dr. Ray Nebel, Lon Peters, Bill Young and more recently joined by Todd Kranz, together with their teams are committed to the highest quality service for members and customers around the world. Their teams in order fulfillment, SMS, SRS, and sales teams throughout the world have grown Select Sires to new heights not thought possible by previous generations. And finally, my executive assistant, Jackie Salyer and her team keep this organization running smoothly. Our future will be based on our ability to bring leaders like this to Select Sires to invent, produce and serve our owners in new ways that elevate the industry for generations to come.

From a personal standpoint, I am blessed to work for a great company, a great board and a great group of professionals that share my passions. There are amazing teams like this all throughout the Select Sires federation that make Select Sires what it is today. I am glad to be a part of the Select Sires family.

A Business Model that Works

The success and growth that Select Sires has experienced through the years is often credited to the arrangement of member cooperatives that form the larger entity. Select Sires Inc. exists to centralize semen production, conduct research, develop marketing material and provide program management. The member cooperatives maintain the grassroots and personal connection to the customer with an intimate understanding in the specific needs of the market being served. It is a business model that could work anywhere but it is especially successful with a farmer-owned cooperative as rural America has a history of working together.

Select Sires has had member cooperatives join the federation throughout the 50-year history and member cooperatives have left and combined with other member cooperatives during that same history. Currently, there are nine member cooperatives that form Select Sires. This structure has served as a great model for 50 years and the connection should remain strong for the next 50 years. This is the story of the nine member cooperatives that form Select Sires.

ALL WEST/SELECT SIRES

All West/Select Sires has had a history with Select Sires almost as long as any other cooperative, even though they joined the federation 10 years after Select Sires was originally established. They began in Washington as Skagit County Artificial Breeders in 1941. The cooperative that was to become All West served as a conduit for Select Sires' semen to the west coast before officially becoming a member cooperative.

In early 1968, the board of All West Breeders invited the general manager of Select Sires at the time, Jim Mellinger, to come to a meeting to explain the thoughts and goals of the new federation of cooperatives. Although a decision was made to remain on their own at that time, an agreement was forged in May 1968 to handle semen from Select Sires and provide semen from All West sires to the members of Select Sires for marketing in their areas.

Interest in Select Sires continued with a committee from All West including Archie Nelson, a future general manager of All West, to study the structure and by-laws of Select Sires in mid-1969. Strong sales growth continued for All West and it was becoming increasingly evident that a stronger bond between Select Sires and All West would be mutually beneficial.

In May of 1975, a team of leaders from Select Sires including new General Manager Dick Chichester traveled west to talk to a large group and answer questions about the membership of All West and Select Sires. At the end of that meeting, the decision was made and All West would join the federation of Select Sires as a stock-holding member of the federation. Shortly thereafter, some All West sires took a long ride east to join their soon-to-be stablemates in Ohio as members of the Select Sires line-up and shipments of semen began heading west from Ohio for use by All West. In the first shipment were 890 units of ELEVATION, a door opener in many different ways.

An early collection of semen for All-West Breeders.

Exercising bulls in the early days at Corvalis, Oregon

The affiliation with Select only accelerated the growth that All West was enjoying and other efficiencies were gained by joining Select Sires. Previously, All West had published its own sire directory featuring the sires available from the facility in Burlington, Wash. Now as a member of Select Sires, the cooperative could use the resources and promotional materials of Select Sires and the in-house resources at All West could be reallocated towards additional sales and service personnel to work with the membership.

In late 1973, Superior Sires became distributors of Select Sires semen for most of California. When All West joined Select in 1975, they shared the Superior Sires market and by 1977, Superior Sires of California partnered with All West for California distribution and the cooperative was now responsible for sales of semen from Canada to Mexico. The partnership with the managers of Superior Sires, Tom Olson and Lloyd Vierra, was a productive one. It was an example of a California business joining Select Sires to facilitate marketing of Select Sires semen to an expanded area. Another California business would later become a key marketer of Select Sires semen to a larger market in the form of World Wide Sires.

The late 1970s and early 1980s were a boom time for semen sales and service in the All West/Select Sires marketing area. Select Sires bulls were household names and the explosion of west coast dairy production created a perfect environment for growth of the cooperative. By now all bulls had moved to Ohio from the Burlington facility and semen production was no longer occurring at All West facilities.

The new Turlock, California facility nearing completion in 1995

The 10th anniversary of Select Sires membership in 1985 and attaining the longtime goal of selling one-half million units in 1984 led to a large celebration for All West. The good times kept on rolling as even a herd reduction program that saw 200,000 cows exit in 1987 could not dampen sales at All West. Sires such as BLACKSTAR and MARS TONY were hitting their prime and strong west coast sales of Select Sires semen helped to build new production facilities back in Ohio at the time. Sales growth continued in the 1990s and another milestone was just missed in 1993 when 747,543 units were sold at All West, the best sales year ever to that point.

In 1995, a new All West facility in at Turlock, Calif. was built and interest in bulls like MATHIE and INTEGRITY was heavy in the All West sales area. Animal products were becoming a bigger presence in All West's marketing efforts and in 1997, for the first time in history, All West marketed over $7 million of semen. This record would only last for a little while as the year 2000 saw another record with over $8.5 million in semen sales and $2.2 million in product sales leading to the construction of a new Burlington facility in 2001. Record sales years had become an annual occurrence at this point and product sales also became a key part of the revenue for the cooperative. All West/Select Sires set another sales record in 2014 with a 4.2% growth rate seeing 1,944,833 units marketed by the cooperative.

Key leadership at All West included Archie Nelson who retired as general manager of the cooperative in 1991 after 28 years of service and Herald Catlin who served as general manager from 1991 until 2009, when current General Manager, Jim Wells, was appointed as his replacement.

COBA/SELECT SIRES INC.

COBA/Select Sires Inc. is the only cooperative that formed Select Sires to remain in its original structure. Founded in Columbus, Ohio in 1946, the Central Ohio Breeding Association (COBA) joined with Kentucky Artificial Breeding Association (KABA), Northern Illinois Breeding Cooperative (NIBCO) and Southern Illinois Breeding Association (SIBA) to form Select Sires in 1965. When COBA began in 1946, it was the combination of two smaller associations; the Northeast Ohio Breeding Association and the Western Ohio Breeders Association. To consolidate operations, a 113-acre farm was purchased seven miles west of Columbus, Ohio and the COBA facilities are still on this property today. The early days of COBA saw most distribution of semen occur through technician channels and in 1954 the cooperative began breeding cows in Texas. COBA established operations in Tyler, Texas to handle the additional distribution and from there, shipments began to Colorado, Montana, New Mexico and even the first foray into Mexico.

Richard H. Kellogg, former general manager of COBA, had a desire to sample additional young sires available for the members of his cooperative. On a snowy night in February 1961, the first of many meetings that would lead to the formation of Select Sires was held in Indianapolis, Ind. with leaders of the two Illinois breeding cooperatives. The focus of the meeting was how the groups could work together to help their individual members.

COBA was in need of semen, as a few of their Holstein bulls had suddenly stopped producing. A college friendship between Kellogg and Wilbur Goeke, the manager of NIBCO, proved fruitful when an agreement was struck for NIBCO to send 6,000

The 1953 trade show display listed many reasons that still hold true for Select Sires today.

units of a high-profile Holstein sire to COBA for their use. It was the beginning of a semen-sharing arrangement that would soon also include KABA. On July 1, 1962, COBA began a semen exchange with the other three cooperatives. This arrangement formalized the pricing and agreement for the group to move semen between each other and also accomplished the goal of sharing sampling costs on all breeds except Holstein. Meetings of the exchange group continued and it was soon evident that the group needed to work together even more. The question was what would be the best method for formalizing the arrangement.

By 1964, the four founding members of Select Sires had put a plan in place to consolidate production facilities and organize marketing into one sire directory. Meetings continued and 1965 saw the agreement to put the four groups together in a more formalized company occur. Prior to the agreement, COBA had used a barn sign at the time with a silhouette of a bull above the phrase "home of selected sires." The group liked the concept of sires specially "selected" for use but felt that "Select" did an even better job of getting that point across. In 1957, COBA started to use the name "Select Sires" and the name Select Sires was chosen and adopted as a fitting name for the new formation of cooperatives. The familiar diamond logo also came out of a COBA staff meeting. During a lull in a COBA management meeting, employee Don McKean got to doodling with interlocking "S" designs within a diamond shape. It was simple enough to reflect the family atmosphere that has been a hallmark of Select Sires, yet distinctive enough to show the dedication to customer success that goes with the brand and it has been one of agriculture's more identifiable logos since its adoption in 1965.

COBA/Select Sires' current sales coverage area includes a large portion of the American Southwest and Mexico. When additional sales territory was formally added in the late 1970s and early 1980s, Dr. Wallace Erickson took steps to ensure that COBA was a true cooperative; paying patronage and having member-owners represent the cooperative in all areas. COBA reworked the bylaws to reflect the changes including a name change from Central Ohio Breeding Association to COBA/Select Sires Inc. and a move to have a more manageable customer representative size from 56 Ohio county board members to a 15-member board of directors representing all areas covered by the cooperative.

COBA has also been at the forefront of bringing technology into use for employees and to benefit customers. COBA introduced the handheld computer for use by Select Mating Service (SMS) personnel in 1984, greatly improving the efficiency and effectiveness of SMS evaluators. Rex Castle and a team of COBA evaluators worked closely with Ron Long from Select Sires to help accomplish this time-saving program. COBA also introduced a computer-based sales data-keeping program to assist sales representatives at the point of sale. Both of these technologies went on to be used by additional members of the Select Sires federation. The long history of COBA and its key involvement with

Select Sires also gives an indication of the changing scope of America's dairy and beef landscape. The 1951 COBA Herd Builders catalog contained 112 pages, cost 8 cents to mail and included 285 photos on the seven Ayrshire sires, five Brown Swiss, 12 Guernseys, 11 Holsteins, 10 Jerseys, four Angus sires, four Hereford sires and three Shorthorn sires. The 1965 bull book that combined sires together under the new Select Sires moniker was a 20-page catalog that featured 36 Holsteins, 10 Guernseys, nine Jerseys, seven Brown Swiss, three Ayrshires, two Milking Shorthorns, eight Angus sires, four Charolais sires, seven Polled Herefords, one Horned Hereford, two Shorthorns, one Santa Gertrudis and one Brahman. Today, a COBA/Select Sires Inc. customer has access to at least three different directories: Holstein, High-Components and Beef.

Which Calf Has The Best Chance To Make You Money?

Miss Misfit (Left)

Miss COBA (Right)

MISS MISFIT was sired by "the stockyard bull." (That is he should have been "stockyard bound" as a veal calf.) There were no production records on either her sire or dam to indicate she might be a good producer.

The owner of Miss Misfit measures his cows production by the full milk pail method. Miss Misfit's dam gave only a third of a pail twice a day. But he's a gambler by nature. There's a rabbit's foot in his pocket while he waits for Miss Misfit to come into production. How can he hazard a guess as to what she'll produce, not having any records? Many Miss Misfits are never meant for herd replacements, but they end up there.

MISS COBA . . . She holds real promise of being a moneymaker for her owner William Van Schoyck. Her sire is Carnation Governor Prosperity, Silver Medal Production Sire at COBA. His 24 daughters (her paternal sisters) average 14,114 pounds of milk and 536 pounds of butterfat. On the average they produced 1699 pounds of milk and 101 pounds of fat more than their dams.

Her dam is Ormsby Pontiac Mercedes Lady who has a six-year-old record in 351 days of 22,044 pounds of milk and 868 pounds of fat on twice-daily milking. The fee for breeding this cow to this great sire was only $6. Wasn't this a real bargain?

The chance is "Miss Misfit" will lose money for her owner "Miss COBA" has an excellent chance to be a great moneymaker

THE SIGN OF

BETTER FARMING

BETTER LIVING

COBA SELECTED SIRES

BETTER CATTLE

COBA Service Doesn't Cost — It Pays! Contact Your County Agent or COBA Technician for more information or service —

CENTRAL OHIO BREEDING ASSOCIATION
Serving 57 Ohio Counties

Early COBA advertising showed the advantages of powerful genetics and introduced "Selected Sires" to the customer

Looking at the sales and revenue numbers through the years suggest that helping form Select Sires in 1965 has served the member-owners of COBA/Select Sires very well. The year after Select Sires was formed (1965), COBA sold 248,578 units of semen and had a total revenue of $1,551,446. By Select Sires' 25th anniversary in 1990, COBA sold 544,128 units of semen and had a total revenue of $6,254,245. In terms of market share in 1990, COBA sold about 40 units of semen for every 100 dairy cows in our U.S. geographic service area. In 2001, COBA surpassed 1 million units of semen sold for the first time in its history. Thanks to the high genetic quality and highly fertile semen

7HO7466 Robthom MOSCOW stands in front of a COBA Select Sires truck in Ohio.

provided by Select Sires and the helpful member service programs that were developed, by 2013 COBA's sales had increased to 1,972,303 units of semen representing more than 110 units of semen sold for every 100 dairy cows and gross revenue of $25,227,970.

Because of its proximity to Select Sires, COBA has always had its share of talented employees that have worked for both organizations. The author of the history book of the first 25 years of Select Sires, Bernie Heisner, took the reins of general manager of COBA/ Select Sires on July 1, 1993 replacing the retiring Larry Neel. Heisner remained in that position until his retirement in August 2013. At that time, Duane Logan, former marketing director for the company was appointed as his successor. Logan was a former board member for COBA/Select Sires Inc. while he was actively dairy farming and was on the board at the time of Heisner's selection and appointment. In its 68-year history, COBA has only had five general managers; the aforementioned Heisner and Logan along with Dick Kellogg from 1946 to 1977, Wallace Erickson, Ph.D., from 1977-1988, and Larry Neel from 1988 to 1993. Mr. Neel had his own 41-year career with the cooperative. Also of note are two COBA members that have been president of the board of directors for Select Sires with special connection to the cooperative. Fred Friday was at the helm from 1984 to 1989 and was the breeder of 7HO191 WAYNE-Spring Fond Apollo while Charles Moellendick was president at the turn of the millennium and led the selection committee when new General Manager and CEO David Thorbahn was appointed.

COBA/Select Sires Inc. mission statement is: "COBA/Select Sires Inc. operates as a true cooperative to provide superior genetics and service to benefit its member-customers." That statement has pretty much been in its same form since the beginning of COBA and it is the guidance that directs COBA employees to serve their membership. The history of the Central Ohio Breeding Association intertwines with the history of Select Sires like no other cooperative. Farmers involved with the formation of Select Sires will tell you that getting the structure in place was no easy task. That work and structure arose from humble beginnings to become a genetics and reproductive powerhouse serving customers around the globe. It is a testament to the dedication and focus of farmers from the heartland of America.

EAST CENTRAL/ SELECT SIRES

The beginnings of East Central/Select Sires occurred in 1941 with the establishment of the East Central Breeders Association Cooperative (ECBAC). The cooperative, based in Waupun, Wis., began service with coverage of six counties in southern Wisconsin and partial coverage in four additional counties. Operations began in a rented farm in the city of Waupun. The first breeds were Holstein, Guernsey and Angus, and Dr. E. H. Doudna was the first manager-inseminator, as at that time inseminators had to be veterinarians. The number of cows bred with ECBAC semen in the first year totaled 5,918. Five years later, this amount grew to 13,008 and Dr. Edwin R. Carlson was promoted from cattle breeding and laboratory work to general manager of ECBAC.

In 1951, 10 years after their establishment, ECBAC bred 47,311 cows and built a new bull barn and office building on the same property they're located at today. In their 20th year, ECBAC bred more than 85,000 cows, and in 1965, Alton Dale Block was hired as general manager after Carlson's unexpected death.

Beginning in 1959 and continuing through the early 70s, ECBAC started a pilot project in the artificial insemination of swine, making them one of the early leaders in the swine A.I. industry. Through the research efforts of General Manager Dr. Wallace E. Erickson, frozen boar semen became a reality. His results allowed East Central to sell their swine technology and the cooperative's lineup of genetically superior boars to United Suppliers of Eldora, Iowa in 1975.

In 1976, Erickson announced his resignation to become manager of COBA/Select Sires, causing leaders within the cooperative to explore their best options for the cooperative's future. In addition to finding new leadership, this charge also included finding avenues for adding additional bull power to the lineup available to East Central members. Tri-State Breeders and Mid-West Breeders were two of the options suggested but a lot of the membership kept discussing ELEVATION, the breed leader available from Select Sires.

High seller in the 1979 Select Sale was Kam-Ja Glendell Lena selling for $26,000.

President of the board of ECBAC at the time, Clarence Boyke, made it clear that EL-EVATION was the biggest driver in the desire of ECBAC to join the Select Sires family. The membership was anxious to expand the lineup of sires available beyond 35 sires and bull power was a real desire of the cooperative membership. After a couple of previous courtship attempts that were not fruitful, Dick Chichester invited East Central's leadership to come to Ohio in early 1977. This led to East Central becoming a member cooperative of Select Sires. On May 1, 1977 East Central joined the Select Sires family, a truly historic day when 110 delegates voted and only three opposed to joining Select Sires. At this time, all the ECBAC bulls left for Ohio and the Waupun facilities were home to only young sires in waiting.

Following the historic merger, William Thompson took over as general manager and, under his leadership, ECBAC continued business as a member cooperative of Select Sires. In 1979 and 1983, ECBAC hosted "The Select Sale," held at World Dairy Expo. These sales showcased cattle from ECBAC's area and also included young-sire daughters from across the country. These sales helped promote Select Sires around the world.

In 1984, ECBAC members voted to change the cooperative name to East Central/Select Sires (EC/SS) and in 1991, during their 50th year, the EC/SS board of directors named Alan R. Deming as the new general manager. Deming, at that time a 13-year veteran of the cooperative, took the reins after former General Manager Thompson accepted a new position at Select Sires in Ohio. EC/SS recorded 173,816 services and 325,506 units sold in 1991. During the mid-90s, all remaining bulls at EC/SS were moved to Ohio and a warehouse was created at the Waupun facilities to hold an inventory of various cow-management products. In 2000, when Select Sires and Sire Power joined forces to form the largest A.I. organization in the U. S., EC/SS was able to hire five new Sire Power employees and annual sales grew by an additional 50,000 units.

Today, East Central/Select Sires covers the southern 23 counties in Wisconsin with headquarters on the same property they built facilities on in 1951. As the smallest geographic member of Select Sires, East Central runs their business in a way unique to other member cooperatives of the federation. The high density of cow population allows EC/SS to roll-out new innovations fairly quickly and the cooperative has been a proving ground for new technologies and techniques that have benefitted the rest of the Select Sires federation.

Tail-chalking is one of these techniques developed at EC/SS. In 1999, with a highly trained technician force of more than 60 technicians and a customer base that needed additional services, the whole-herd concept of technician service began and has served East Central's membership well; growing from zero services in 1999 to 240,000 services in 2013.

Another technology that has really grown in the service area of East Central has been

Current General Manager Al Deming, second from right, joins member service representative Tom Budde, middle, in celebrating his 100,000th first-service insemination.

the relatively new adoption of cow-monitoring systems for detecting estrus, temperature, activity, rumination, eating time, resting time and cow location. Again, a high-density customer area coupled with employees that really understand the technology and software has allowed EC/SS to become a cooperative leader in the number of systems placed and serviced.

After 72 years of business, total unit sales at EC/SS in 2013 were 521,010 units, and their strong group of technicians had 366,965 services. Operating revenue was $13,318,501 assets grew by 4.8 percent from the previous year, and net margin grew by 4.29 percent, while growth in diversified products saw an 11 percent increase over 2012.

SELECT SIRES MIDAMERICA INC.

Select Sires MidAmerica Inc. is technically the newest member cooperative of Select Sires, but the cooperatives that joined to form it have a history almost as long as artificial insemination does. MidAmerica is the result of a merger between Cache Valley Select Sires and Kentucky Artificial Breeding Association (KABA), which occurred January 1, 2012. KABA was one of the original founding members of Select Sires, while Cache Valley joined Select Sires shortly after that in 1969. Each member stayed as an independent member cooperative of Select Sires until both cooperatives realized that similar markets and opportunity for economies of scale could provide a stronger joined cooperative.

KABA was incorporated in 1945, and managed by Marshall Carpenter. It was an ear-

Customer Don Thornley stands with two men that would lead the cooperative, Ferron Perkes and Randy Hill.

ly pioneer in the expansion of A.I. services to the dairy and beef producers of Kentucky. Enjoying a close relationship with the University of Kentucky, whose extension agents were charged with "expanding the wide distribution of superior germ plasma of carefully chosen dairy cattle bulls and to provide for developing improved methods of carrying on the work of artificial breeding and to train

Olympic Gold Medalist Rulon Gardner stands with his father Reed Gardner, a longtime technician, distributor, and board member.

master technicians." It was valuable service like this that allowed KABA to grow and become an integral member of the Kentucky dairy industry. It also was a reason for their involvement in a landmark research trial published in the 1954 Journal of Animal Science that used KABA data from 1950 to establish correlations between milk production and breeding efficiencies in dairy cattle.

The Cache Valley Breeding Association (CVBA) was incorporated in 1948 with help from the Utah State University and extension service after a group of dairy producers from the Cache Valley saw the need to improve the genetics of their herds. CVBA bred their first cow on December 1, 1948. The longtime manager instrumental in the move to Select Sires was J. Elmo Packer, who served as general manager from 1948 through 1972. The 1950s were a rewarding time of growth for CVBA, but the movement to frozen semen in the 1960s instilled a need to look at other options that allowed CVBA to be competitive and provide additional breeding options to its membership. As president of the board, Ronald Hawkes was most instrumental in CVBA joining Select Sires. His tireless work in realizing productive gains through a relationship with Select Sires resulted in Cache Valley joining the federation on August 1, 1969.

The continuity of leadership in all member cooperatives for Select Sires remains notable. For example, Cache Valley came into existence in 1949 and four leaders served as general manager during that time, J. Elmo Packer from 1949 to 1972, Rulon Osmond from 1972 to 1980, Ferron Perkes from 1980 to 2005 and Randy Hill from 2005 to present day, as the manager of Select Sires MidAmerica. When asked about the merger between Cache Valley and KABA, General Manager Hill mentioned, "A big reason why we merged is because our member area markets weren't like each other. We had a strong connection in beef but the boards of the two groups realized that we could better

The Select Sires MidAmerica office building in Logan, Utah as it appeared in 2001

utilize the total genetic offerings of Select Sires by combining our groups. The allocation gained by a combined group allowed semen to be transferred to parts of our marketing area that could best use it."

It was a logical combination that had roots in the mid-1980s when the Cache Valley cooperative gained the marketing areas of South Dakota and Nebraska from Select Sires. Ferron Perkes was general manager at the time and the addition of Nebraska made the geographic connection to KABA's marketing area of Missouri. The new partnership of Select Sires MidAmerica Inc. is responsible for 35 percent of the domestic beef sales at Select Sires and it has been helped by investments made by the new member cooperative that could not have been afforded if the former cooperatives were still on their own.

Select Sires MidAmerica Inc. has been one of the faster growing members of Select Sires in the years leading up to the 50th anniversary. Capitalizing on growth in the dairy industry that has occurred in regions covered by the cooperative, Select Sires MidAmerica has been able to supplement the outstanding beef coverage already in place in traditional areas serviced to add a strong dairy presence in states like Idaho. This growth has occurred with strong leadership connected to the customer-owner of the cooperative. When Cache Valley and KABA came together, Cache Valley General Manager Hill was named general manager of the new Select Sires MidAmerica organization and Paul Kunkel was named assistant general manager after a long stint as general manager of KABA. Both gentlemen have had long-standing connections to Select Sires service. Hill still maintains a sales route in his local area to stay connected to the customer and Kunkel joined KABA after a long period of service to the beef department at Select Sires.

In 1990, the combined sales of Cache Valley and KABA totaled 391,097 units and both cooperatives were coming off of record-setting years. In 2014, the combined MidAmerica regions sold over 1.3 million units in the same sales area. Select Sires is built on the foundation of member-owners looking for new ways to cooperate. An original member of Select Sires, KABA joined a long-time member cooperative from the first major expansion in 1969, and it is the MidAmerica member that has benefitted.

MINNESOTA SELECT SIRES CO-OP, INC.

Minnesota Select Sires Co-op, Inc. has had a serendipitous path to success. In the mid-1970s, Select Sires formalized the sales efforts for the state and region by creating the North Central Division. Marketing Director for Select Sires Inc., George Miller, hired a few people and instructed them to go out and drum-up business. It was fertile ground for growth and the area quickly grew and additional sales and service representatives were needed for continued success. In 1981, Lyle Kruse was hired as a sales representative covering parts of North and South Dakota before becoming the supervisor of a larger sales force for the North Central Division in 1982. Sales growth was still strong but customers were often disappointed that they could not get all the semen that they wanted as a result of the area not being a member cooperative of Select Sires. Steps began to change that.

As discussion of forming a member cooperative grew in Minnesota and surrounding states, a fortunate turn of events added to the sales and services that the company could provide. In late 1984, several technicians from Minnesota Valley Breeders Association (MVBA) reached out to Kruse and the group at Select Sires about joining the team. Discussions continued and one final informational meeting was held with 20 MVBA technicians in attendance. Fifteen of those technicians decided to join the Select Sires team and the North Central Division instantly became the top service provider in the area along with the semen sales that were already strong and growing. It was a strong step towards becoming a full member cooperative of Select Sires.

The group of technicians that got it all rolling in 1984.

The first General Manager of Minnesota Select Sires, Lyle Kruse.

A steering committee and planning meetings accelerated efforts in 1985 to take the steps necessary for membership in Select Sires. At the time the Select Sires rule was that an area must have been selling 40 units per 100 cows to qualify for a new area. Even though the Minnesota division was not quite there, it was obvious that the team would get there fairly quickly, especially given the new employees that were serving customers. Duane Berg from Annandale, Minn. kept leading the charge and on January 1, 1986, Minnesota Select Sires became a fully recognized member cooperative of Select Sires. Duane Berg was nominated to be president, a role he held for 12 years, and Lyle Kruse became the general manager, a role he held until going to work for Select Sires Inc. as vice president of U. S. sales in 2008. It was the first time that a member cooperative started from scratch and was not a merger or an existing breeder cooperative.

Steady progress continued to follow Minnesota Select Sires. Beginning in rented facilities, the goal for the leaders of the cooperative was to be debt-free and begin internalizing many of the processes of the cooperative. In 1991, Minnesota Select Sires was debt-free and accounting and record-keeping work previously performed by Select Sires in Ohio was taken over at the home office. The continued success also allowed construction of a new facility in St. Cloud, Minn. in 1993. The central location conveniently serves customers and employees while also allowing continued expansion of specialty premium products.

Minnesota has always been one of the strongest dairy areas in the U.S. and it is fitting that an upstart member of Select Sires should enjoy the growth that the cooperative has experienced. "We couldn't cover the back roads because we only had enough sales force to cover the main roads," said Butch Lerum, an early employee. Today the entire region is blanketed with not only sales people, but a highly trained team of service specialists, mating coordinators and reproductive consultants. Minnesota Select Sires is another example of the Select Sires way; hire good people, train them well and then give them the best product to sell. A Minnesota bull even boosted sales; ELTON became an impact sire for Select Sires and was recognized as such on the Impact Sires artwork in 2011. With ELTON being a close parent in the pedigrees of DURHAM and O MAN the Minnesota genetics provided by ELTON have spread across the world.

In 2008, when Lyle Kruse was named to his new position at Select Sires Inc., Chris Sigurdson was named the second general manager in Minnesota Select Sires' history. Another current leader with a long history of leadership within the cooperative is Myron Czech. Czech is the current chairman of the Select Sires Inc. board of directors. His own farm mirrors many of the farms in the Minnesota Select Sires marketing area; it has grown to a larger size and with a focus on larger volumes of semen from a broader group of sires, with less demand on a few hot sires. That movement has driven the continued demand for the balanced lineup of Select Sires.

A review of the growth at Minnesota Select Sires is noteworthy because it really reflects the growth pattern of much of Select Sires; like-minded individuals get together and desire a better product with better services. The group then figures out a way to get it done and the growth is a reward for the effective process and hard work. In 1983, the North Central Division of Select Sires sold 87,000 units and $1,010,000 of semen in a four-state area. Just six years later, sales had doubled to $2,328,956 of semen sales in 1989. In 2007, the growth had continued to 376,925 units and $5,365,286. Most recent sales figures from 2013 show continued growth to 418,889 units and the next semen sales goal of $6 million.

The Minnesota Select Sires office built in 1993.

NorthStar Cooperative is probably the most diverse member cooperative of Select Sires. Beginning in Michigan in 1944 as a product of the Michigan Extension Service, the Michigan Artificial Breeders Cooperative (MABC) capitalized on interest in A.I. across the state to begin local breeding associations that could benefit from centralized bull management. Eleven locals were formed and May 31, 1944 saw the first shipment of semen go from MABC to the local members.

As with many future member cooperatives of Select Sires, MABC was utilizing fresh semen in the 1950s and was experiencing tremendous growth. A move into other species in the early 1960s caused a name change from Michigan Artificial Breeders Cooperative to Michigan Animal Breeders Cooperative, but the demand for other species never took off and the focus again turned to cattle. An agreement was made in 1963 on behalf of the board to begin providing frozen semen for customers that desired to inseminate their own animals. This continued a steady growth in demand for product and services causing MABC to look for additional resources to market, even though cow numbers in Michigan were declining.

The cooperative joined the United Semen Exchange in 1965, allowing additional sires to be marketed to the membership. This provided an economical source of additional bull power. After federation studies from 1967 to 1969, MABC was interested in joining Select Sires. In his travels, Clint Meadows, Ph.D., had experienced many different A.I.

This 1950's trade show display showed Michigan dairy producers how easy it was to retire the bull.

The AI Training Center for the cooperative in Lansing, Michigan.

cooperative structures and realized that Select Sires had a structure and set of goals that meshed with MABC. On May 21, 1968, a group of MABC leaders met with Select Sires and learned about the federation of cooperatives including the young sire program. It captured the attention of the MABC group and they contacted other United Semen Exchange members to form a Federation Feasibility Study Group to gauge their interest in joining the fledgling cooperative of Select Sires.

There was considerable agreement among the members in the Feasibility Study Group and after a follow-up meeting in Washington D.C. on May 28 and 29, 1968 the breeding cooperatives of MABC, Mississippi ABA, East Tennessee ABA, Tennessee ABA and Cache Valley agreed to join Select Sires. On June 23, MABC became a member of Select Sires and July 1 was the first day of operations under the new arrangement. MABC's decision to join Select Sires came 25 years after it was first organized in 1944.

The arrangement breathed new life into MABC and the savings and efficiencies gained by being a member of Select Sires helped to strengthen membership interest in the cooperative, even though MABC was now a marketing and sales cooperative and no longer a bull stud.

By 1973, an additional sales area in Indiana had been added to MABC. The northern Wisconsin sales area was added to MABC membership area in 1975 with Northwestern Wisconsin joining the territory in 1977. The added area helped sales to grow and it was becoming evident that a new headquarters would be needed, leading to the purchase of 10 acres outside of Michigan State University's campus in 1977.

The 1980s were a period of up-and-down sales for MABC, just as the dairy industry was experiencing its own case of up-and-down results. In 1982 MABC changed its name to MABC Select Sires. In 1980 the greatest sales gain in MABC's history led to an all-time high for sales in the cooperative of 522,246 units in 1985. The dairy herd buyout program came in 1986 however, and MABC saw 2,800 producer bids accepted in the MABC marketing area, which was a huge blow to the cooperative. Michigan alone lost 12 percent of fluid milk production through the program. This meant that three years after setting a record for unit sales, a 10-year low for sales would occur with 474,000 units being marketed in 1988. The trying times and poor dairy economy caused MABC to explore a merger with East Central/ Select Sires in the late 1980s but differing goals of the cooperatives did not lead to a deal.

The 1990s saw a return to sales growth for MABC Select Sires with sales again growing to over 500,000 units. Longtime Manager Kenneth Baushke became ill, leading to his retirement in 1991. Mike Bills, a former sales representative for MABC that had gone on to lead personnel training and development for Select Sires Inc. in Ohio returned to MABC as the general manager in 1992. New leadership and a continued demand for efficiency saw MABC flatten out its sales and management structure in the mid-1990s. Customer focus groups began and provided important information about what the MABC customer most needed from their cooperative which led to additional structural changes.

Overwhelming support to change the name to NorthStar Cooperative came in 1994. It provided a better fit for the desire of the cooperative to provide a range of services and to show the renewed focus on customer service. In 1996 NorthStar restructured to a stock- based cooperative, the pension plan was redone and strategic planning was implemented to explore additional opportunities in 1997, Gary Smith (later named general manager in 2003) led a movement towards additional products as leader of the Ag Products and Technologies Unit and 1997 also saw the addition of DHI services to NorthStar. The next year, UniStar was created to allow NorthStar to own for-profit companies while protecting the cooperative status at the core. BioStar Research, now Antel Biosystems, was one of the first products of that move towards offering additional services. General Manager Smith's announced retirement on March 31, 2015 led the cooperative to name Mark Adam, the director of integrated services for the cooperative, as his successor.

PRAIRIE STATE/ SELECT SIRES

Prairie State has had a circuitous route of Select Sires membership. In 1965, the formation of Select Sires saw a combination of COBA, KABA and two Illinois breeding cooperatives (Northern Illinois Breeding Cooperative and Southern Illinois Breeding Association). The two Illinois cooperatives had been pioneers of introducing artificial insemination techniques to the heartland and had seen tremendous growth in their service areas. Before joining Select Sires, the two cooperatives, which began in the 1940s, had inseminated over 180,000 cows using A.I. on 50,000 Illinois farms by 1953. It was a logical step for them to join the federation of cooperatives forming Select Sires in an effort to share additional bull power and technical expertise. It was also logical to eventually join forces for a strong Illinois presence which they did by forming the Illinois Breeding Cooperative (IBC) on March 1, 1968.

IBC remained a member of the Select Sires federation until it formally withdrew its participation from the federation on July 31, 1973. Members of the Select Sires family have had their share of disagreements, especially early on in the formative years before rules, both written and unwritten, were established. It was a challenge to these rules that caused IBC to leave Select Sires. The general manager of IBC felt that their production stalls for producing Select Sires semen in Illinois carried additional value and

An early educational session at NIBCO helped to expand the understanding of reproductive techniques.

General Manager Devin Albrecht begins a training session with Dan Den Herder

recommended to their board to negotiate better rates from Select Sires. When those efforts turned out to be less than fruitful, IBC pulled out of the federation and began purchasing semen from the Curtiss Breeding Service, a private A.I. company headquartered in Illinois. The relationship between Curtiss and IBC never materialized the way that IBC had hoped and lasted just six years.

After IBC pulled out of the federation, newly appointed Select Sires General Manager Dick Chichester had to act fast to try and keep Select Sires' presence strong in the key Illinois market. The Illinois/Wisconsin division of Select Sires started on August 1, 1973 headed by a former IBC employee, Ray Hess. That first month saw two technicians and one direct herd salesman sell $5,673 of monthly revenue. The focus on genetics and service that Select Sires was quickly being recognized for did help grow the new Illinois/Wisconsin sales division as 12 technicians and three direct herd salesmen were bringing in over $40,000 of monthly revenue by the end of the year.

The success of the Illinois/Wisconsin division continued and by 1978, customers purchasing semen from the division of Select Sires were anxious to be re-admitted to the cooperative. A move to membership would allow additional control over the destiny of the group and allow them to receive patronage like the other member organizations. Chichester attended customer meetings in Illinois in 1978 designed to lay groundwork for potentially adding this sales area back into Select Sires as a member cooperative. At those meetings, three options became evident as possibilities for the Illinois/Wisconsin customers: 1. Stay as they were, 2. Put the northern part of Illinois into East Central/Select Sires and the southern part into KABA Select Sires or 3. Form a new cooperative. The consensus coming out of the meetings was to form a new cooperative. It was also brought up at the meetings that a call should be made to IBC as the rumors in Illinois were that IBC had not fared well since leaving Select Sires.

Ron Debatin, a Holstein breeder from Illinois with strong interest in seeing their area gain membership in Select Sires, reached out to IBC and was quickly rebuffed. The rejection was short-lived however, as IBC called back within a few weeks to explore the possibilities of once again affiliating with Select Sires. Representatives of the groups were invited to attend the 1979 annual meeting and Chichester worked with the two groups to find common ground. It was evident during the meeting that IBC did not have the position or desire to do much bargaining and a new cooperative was approved for membership. Financing to purchase a position in Select Sires was arranged through the St. Louis Bank for Cooperatives and Prairie State/Select Sires brought original membership of Select Sires back into the federation on August 21, 1979.

Prairie State/Select Sires has been a key contributor to the success of Select Sires ever since readmission. Its geographic location often serves as a gateway to the west both in American history and in the marketing efforts of Select Sires. The facility in Hampshire, Ill. has allowed Select Sires to balance production cycles with additional animal stalls while also providing additional semen units to meet growing demand, mainly in the beef markets. From November 1980 through 2011, Prairie States capitalized on their production facility by producing semen for a collection of German groups called ORE-CO. The group, which eventually transformed into Top Q, would purchase North American genetics and send semen back to Germany for use on German farms. Genomics made it hard for the German group to keep that cost effective. After being approached by Select Sires in January 2012 to assist in semen production for additional needs of the cooperative, the decision was made by May 2012 to begin supplementing Select Sires production needs with the facility at Hampshire. In 2014, 40 beef sires made their home at Prairie State/Select Sires, greatly enhancing semen availability on some key beef sires.

Prairie State's customers have always had a strong interest in the latest genetics. Many top breeders reside in the membership area and this was one of the driving reasons why the group wanted to help form Select Sires and why they eventually rejoined the cooperative. Since the advent of genomics, Prairie State has always had a high percentage of their sales from Super Samplers™ (the best genomic young sires), showing an interest by the member-owners in acquiring the best new genetics available in the marketplace. It is no surprise that breeders from the area have an interest in breeding great cattle, as Devin Albrecht, general manager since the 2009 retirement of Mike Goggin, mentions that Prairie State's breeders supplied half of the Holstein sires featured in the Select Sires impact sires artwork. In 2013, the print was updated to feature 14 sires and seven of them were bred in Prairie State membership area: 7HO477 GLENDELL, 7HO980 MARK, 7HO1897 BLACKSTAR, 7HO3948 EMORY, 7HO5157 DURHAM, 7HO6417 O MAN and 7HO7004 DAMION.

SELECT SIRE POWER INC.

The merger that brought Select Sire Power Inc. into existence was one of the first big moves of the David Thorbahn era as chief executive officer of Select Sires Inc. Established in 1950 as Virginia Animal Breeders, the marriage that brought the A.I. cooperative Sire Power into the Select Sires family took some creative management and expansion of membership area to complete. When Select Sire Power was officially a newly formed member cooperative of Select Sires Inc. on July 1, 2000, it became the third largest member of the federation.

The Virginia Artificial Breeders Association was formed in February 1950 when the Northern Virginia Cooperative Breeding Association and the Blue Ridge Artificial Breeding Association realized that the dairy farmers of Virginia would be best served by one organization that could serve the entire state. The Blue Ridge office located in Rocky Mount, Va., was deemed the logical choice for the new entity and this office still remains in use by Select Sire Power to this day.

The first general manager of the cooperative was William Armstrong. He hired a young George A. Miller to become a field man for the stud in 1956. In 1973, George would go on to be the long-time director of marketing and development for Select Sires after serving eight years as manager for Virginia Artificial Breeders Association. In 1957, Armstrong would hire Emory Brubaker, another future general manager of the cooperative. A pattern of leadership and succession had begun.

The Sire Power purchase in 2000 delivered additional production capability. This main production area and the Valley View facility added additional housing for approximately 500 sires.

These sires are awaiting their next meal at the Ebersole Center, one of the facilities gained in the Sire Power acquisition and named for long time Sire Department Manager at Sire Power, J. Lloyd Ebersole.

Armstrong remained general manager until 1965. At that time, Miller was named manager and took many steps that would lay the groundwork for joining Select Sires. The first moves were joining the United Semen Exchange, a collection of cooperatives owning young and proven sires that formed a network of future Select Sires member cooperatives, and total utilization of frozen semen. Another decision by Miller that proved rewarding for Select Sires was the employment of Clif Marshall in 1968 to be a field supervisor/laboratory assistant. (Marshall later traveled with the bulls to Michigan when bull housing was consolidated in 1973 and supervised semen production for Select Sires in Ohio.) A final hire by George Miller in 1973 was Wayne Dudley to expand a custom collection program; Dudley also would become a general manager of the cooperative.

Supplemental semen from United Semen Exchange and other cooperatives filled current needs for Virginia ABA, but a more permanent arrangement was sought. In 1967, Virginia and Maryland-West Virginia leaders met with potential federation members. One of the first meetings saw representatives from Eastern A.I. Cooperative and Select Sires attend to communicate what each group could offer. Additional meetings occurred and the board of directors did much due diligence. Subsequent meetings revealed that Select Sires had the legal structure of the two groups that allowed quick entry into Select Sires Inc. Dr. Jim Nichols, at that time head of Virginia Tech's dairy science department and an architect of the plan, said going into the meeting, "…the group will not join Select Sires for what they are today, but for what the total group can be with a new organization." Decision day came on May 28, 1969 and a unanimous vote was cast to join Select Sires.

Now that Virginia ABA was a member of Select Sires, a movement began to adopt the successful business model that Virginia ABA had used to grow the business and take that model into additional geographical sales areas. This plan began in September 1969 with the addition by Select Sires of eastern North Carolina to the cooperative. Virginia connections to Select Sires have been numerous throughout the years. Two of the four general managers that Select Sires has known, Dr. Jim Nichols and Dick Chichester, both have strong Virginia and Virginia Tech connections. When the latter was named general manager in 1973, he recruited George Miller to join him. This led to Emory Brubaker being named general manager of Virginia ABA Select Sires on October 1, 1973. The trend of territory expansion continued and Florida was added to the marketing area of the cooperative in 1977. At this time the name was also changed to Virginia-North Carolina (VA-NC) Select Sires. Brubaker oversaw a great deal of additional territorial expansion including Maryland, West Virginia and Delaware in 1985, and Pennsylvania and New Jersey in 1992. His first hire was Norm Vincel as beef supervisor, another future general manager of Select Sire Power.

When Brubaker retired in 1993, Wayne Dudley became general manager of VA-NC Select Sires. The cooperative continued exceptional sales and profitability growth with patronage dividends becoming a hallmark of VA-NC Select Sires service to its membership. The late 1990s led to additional challenges facing the dairy and beef industry. Not all industry players were as strong as Select Sires and it was becoming evident that

Sales staff gathered at the 50th anniversary of Virginia ABA.

some additional consolidation would occur. Sire Power had previously reached out to Select Sires but a deal never could be consummated. After another planned merger did not come to fruition, Sire Power again explored an opportunity to join Select Sires. This time the key players and assets were more aligned and talks continued to see if a merger could benefit the stakeholders of the organizations.

Sire Power had enjoyed some decent growth of its own during the previous decade. A strong membership base in the Mid-Atlantic States featuring a combination of A.I. cooperatives including Maryland-West Virginia, Northeastern Breeders Association, Lehigh Valley and the first A.I. cooperative in America from New Jersey allowed it to expand the national marketing presence of Sire Power and international marketing was providing a very nice return to the group. As the national sales of Sire Power were starting to grow and provide some payback on the investment in expansion, the global market experienced currency pressures and an erosion of markets that saw international income to Sire Power severely subside. There was too much invested in new markets to walk away from the move to grow the business but it also was going to be a challenge to sustain the investment without the international dollars that had been provided earlier. Sire Power needed to find a partner that could help them to meet the needs of their loyal membership area, but allow them to back off from their investment in national sales expansion. Select Sires would prove to be that white knight.

As the new leader of Select Sires, David Thorbahn recognized the potential growth that still existed for Select Sires in the industry and also realized that some additional facilities would be needed to fuel this growth. The Sire Power group represented an opportunity for Select Sires to continue their trend line of growth and also pick up some needed real estate at the same time. The challenge was that Sire Power had membership marketing area within existing sales area of VA-NC Select Sires. Creativity was needed to make an arrangement work and the Sire Power membership area joined VA-NC Select Sires to form Select Sire Power on July 1, 2000. The national marketing area representatives of Sire Power could then join the other Select Sires member cooperatives serving their area. The final pieces to the partnership included Select Sires purchasing the real estate assets of Sire Power and the non-member marketing area of New York and New England that was previously managed by Select Sires becoming the marketing area of Select Sire Power.

It was a plan that required much thought because there were many different parts and entities involved. In the end, it was another example of a transition of an A.I. cooperative joining the Select Sires family and each of the parties benefitting in the process. The current general manager for Select Sire Power is the aforementioned Norm Vincel who assumed the role on January 1, 2011.

SOUTHEAST SELECT SIRES INC.

Southeast Select Sires Inc. came into existence in its present form on January 1, 1997 when the boards of Southeast Select Sires Inc. and Midsouth/Select Sires Co-Op decided to merge operations. This merger followed the creation of Southeast Select Sires on January 1, 1994 when the cooperatives of East Tennessee Select Sires and Tennessee Artificial Breeding Association joined together. East Tennessee Select Sires can trace its history back to beginnings in 1944 and it is unique in that it has had only two general managers in that entire time, Fred Cowart who was the manager from 1944 to 1981 and Tim Riley, the manager from 1981 to present. That is a remarkable testament to people making the difference at Select Sires.

All three cooperatives that merged together to form Southeast Select Sires were breeding associations comprised of smaller county breeding groups. The southern U.S. has a diverse market of dairy and beef producers and these breeding groups were the main and, in many ways, the only avenue for genetic improvement. The cooperative in its form today still owes a lot of its success and influence to state governments. In Tennessee, the cooperative operated on state land from 1946 to 1982 with a land rent of $1 per year for the 31-acre parcel. When the bull stud was being established, prisoners from the state correctional system were utilized to build the barns and prepare the facilities. General Manager Cowart recounts stories of trips to the local country store to buy bologna and bread to provide to the prisoners at lunchtime. They may very well be the only bull facilities that were built in exchange for sandwiches.

Southeast Select Sires service areas cover a lot of geography and the delivery trucks are a bull stud on wheels. L-R: Todd Lee, Tim Riley, Allen Stickley, Tim Barnes, Rob Speights and Joe Fowler.

General Manager Tim Riley (top right) standing with the board of directors at the annual meeting in 2008

Southeast Select Sires is the only member of the federation to operate as a Mutual Benefit association. The state of Tennessee, where Southeast Select Sires is located, has recognized the importance of having access to the services and products of an efficient genetics company. Thus, the customers of Southeast Select Sires are not traditional member-owners but receive their form of "patronage" as revolving margins rotated back to them every year. This form of business management has been in place since the early 1960s.

The current manager of Southeast Select Sires, Tim Riley, was selected for his post on November 16, 1981. This means that Riley has earned two distinctions amongst managers of the member cooperatives at Select Sires. He was the youngest person ever selected as a general manager and his current tenure of 34 years makes him the longest-serving general manager of a member cooperative. Tim has seen a lot of change in his time at the helm of Southeast Select Sires and its predecessors. The first combination occurred in 1993. Following the departure of Don Ardrey as the manager at East Tennessee Select Sires, George Miller briefly served as interim manager to stabilize the cooperative until the leaders of the group could take proper action to join with Tennessee Artificial Breeding Association. East Tennessee brought valuable property near Knoxville to the table. The East Tennessee board of directors also led the charge to be one of the industry's first cooperatives to convert to 100 percent frozen semen. Early on they embraced developing the heat synchronization program and geared up equipment to provide turnkey services for their members.

The next move was when MidSouth/Select Sires Co-Op joined the group. J. W. Jennings was a strong, long-time leader of the cooperative. Its board members realized that efficiencies would be gained by having their group join Southeast Select Sires as well. Bill McGee from Southeast Select Sires was president of Select Sires Inc., at the time and it led for a smooth transition in putting the groups together. MidSouth Animal Breeders was originally a product of the Mississppi State University and extension service. It was located on the campus and has a story like many other cooperatives in the Select Sires family of being closely tied to organized education.

Southeast Select Sires currently operates in Spring Hill, Tenn. and it has moved as its goals of serving its customers have transitioned. The original Brentwood property complete with bull barns was returned to the state of Tennessee and is currently a public park. The next move was to Franklin, Tenn. where the group operated custom collection from 1982 to 2001 before that property was sold for housing. The current Spring Hill location serves the needs for service and management with present-day Southeast Select Sires handling the best of dairy and beef genetics from Select Sires Inc.

Southeast Select Sires may very well serve as an example of the cooperation amongst Select Sires as well as any member of the group. The South has always had a reputation for hospitality and cooperation. Since the beginnings of working with Select Sires in 1969, the group has constantly evolved and adapted their business model to meet the needs of the customer. It is a fine line to manage the interests of government, public education and the customer. Southeast Select Sires has strong ties to each of those parties and has grown because of the ability to meet the needs of each of those stakeholders.

◆ ◆ ◆

A Sire for Every Desire...and Country

◆ ◆ ◆

If your sales area starts with one county in Wisconsin and grows to 60 countries around the world, you get to witness a lot of differences in cattle production. Joel Mergler has witnessed that revolution. In his 34 years with Select Sires, Mergler has seen the cooperative grow from 3 million units of mostly domestic sales to a company that markets 14 million units around the planet. It is a reflection of the global market that is firmly rooted in the A.I. industry today.

Mergler currently serves as vice president for international sales. Since he started with Select Sires in 1980, he has held a variety of jobs within the company that prepared him for selling in a variety of markets. In some of the countries serviced by Select Sires, the "dairy" cows are more rugged and stocky than American beef cattle. The country wants to produce milk and dairy protein for their growing population and Select Sires' genetics helps them do it. Matching up the goals of the country with the balanced lineup of Select Sires and training them on the methods to achieve optimum reproductive results is what Joel does best.

For Mergler, it all started on a Guernsey dairy in western Ohio. East Central Breeders had just joined Select Sires and were looking for a technician in Wisconsin. This was his

Joel Mergler joins a delegation from China as they learn more about Select Sires bulls and services.

first foray into Select Sires and from there he became a direct herd sales representative, area sales manager and eventually became vice president of training for Select Sires in 1992. The international market continued to grow and Mergler took his current position in 2008 with 90 percent of his time spent on World Wide Sires markets, mostly in the Eastern hemisphere.

As previously mentioned, the global marketplace is diverse and calls for different sires in different parts of the world. In Ireland, the United Kingdom and the Netherlands, the focus is predominantly on sires that have higher components with less focus on milk. In the Middle East and Northern Africa, the main selection criteria is for high milk sires. In Switzerland, the United Kingdom and France, Type is the main focus. Even within countries there is a great deal of variation. This means that the two main areas to focus on to meet the needs of the country are to first have the sires available to match the breeding goals of the country and secondly to have the training and expertise available to meet the reproductive goals of the country.

The move into Canada in the late 1970s was an early precursor of expanding Select Sires influence around the world. The Canadian A.I. units had a very tight grip over marketing in the country in order to hold on to their industry. Mark Comfort reached out to Select Sires to bring semen into Canada and there was a valid concern that the Canadian government would not allow that to happen. Court cases did occur and it took a lawsuit win for Comfort along with Select Sires' help to open the market to U.S. companies. Even with an open market, it took a great deal of hard work to develop sales in Canada including the challenge of limited semen on top sires, overcoming Canadian pride and dealing with some restrictive rules as well. Today, with the strength of Select Sires GenerVations, Canada ranks as one of Select Sires' fastest growing markets. In much the same way, Select Sires do Brasil, a wholly owned-subsidiary of Select Sires in Brazil, has grown rapidly due to a strong network of sales representatives with a connection to the local market.

Geopolitical changes and disruptions also impact the demand for Select Sires and U.S. genetics. An obvious change that disrupts demand is when an importing country no longer sees eye-to-eye with the U.S. government and decides to take genetic business elsewhere. Other less obvious geopolitical changes occur when a political party gains strength in a country and dictates some of the animal husbandry practices that are preferred in the country. For example, the Green Party in Germany has recently gathered strength behind a movement for polled cattle. The political party takes action in government, rallies other interested groups to the cause (in this case animal activist groups) and influences the type of cattle that a country desires, either directly through legislation or indirectly through purchase choices at the farm level.

It is an extension of genetic choices that have been made throughout history. Red

Dave Thorbahn is joined by Lon Peters and Blaine Crosser as Select Sires is awarded the Exporter of the Year award from the state of Ohio in 2008. L-R: Lt. Gov. of Ohio - Lee Fisher, Lon Peters, Blaine Crosser, Dave Thorbahn, Gov. Ted Strickland and Robert Boggs - 2008 Ohio Director of Agriculture.

Dave Thorbahn, Shin Nosawa, Dick Chichester, and Mike Rakes from World Wide Sires gather to discuss the latest genetic needs in Japan.

and White genetics have always been a popular option in Germany, Switzerland, the Netherlands and Eastern Europe including the Czech Republic, Latvia and Russia. A trait popular in some parts of the world that has a limited domestic following is milking speed. U.S. milking facilities and methods have diminished the need to place a high level of selection criteria for this trait while other milking routines around the world benefit from some consideration for milking speed. Another trait that has little value in the United States that carries real weight in Africa, Southeast Asia and India is crossbred cattle that are heat and tick tolerant. This means that a breed such as Girolando, which is a popular selection for sub-tropic climates, may eventually occupy some stalls in the Select Sires barns. This is another example of how advances in one area, such as genomics, can open up stalls for a new offering and a new opportunity to meet additional needs of cattle breeders around the world.

Ultimately it comes down to Select Sires meeting the needs of the markets that World Wide Sires (WWS) services so that WWS can provide a return to the cooperative. Select Sires purchased WWS to gain efficiencies in meeting worldwide demand for Select Sires semen. The ability to market additional Select Sires semen around the world to a global consumer anxious for the quality genetics coming from Select Sires helps the domestic customer by paying overhead and allocating costs for the member-owner.

WWS, owned in a partnership between Select Sires and Accelerated Genetics, has marketed semen in more than 70 countries around the world since the early 1980s and was purchased by the two farmer-owned cooperatives in 2001. WWS works with a network of locally owned cooperatives, privately owned companies and governmental organizations to take Select Sires semen to the end-user on farms in countries across the globe. It is another example of people making the difference for Select Sires.

John Schouten is the CEO for WWS and offers some of the changes that the global market has witnessed since WWS became affiliated with Select Sires. "The key markets are still an important part of international sales and Western Europe, the United Kingdom, Italy, Turkey, Japan and many others have long held a key position for our sales," said Schouten. "Much of our new growth comes from countries that you might expect like China and countries in South Asia and also from countries that might surprise you such as Saudi Arabia and Iran." Schouten credits a distributor conference that is held every two years as a key opportunity for attendees to participate in strategy sessions that focus on the value of A.I. and to look at ways to enhance market share and build relationships within their sales area. The concept of a WWS training facility in the Western U.S. has also led to a similar training center in China. "Selling products and training services are now our parallel priorities," Schouten adds. "Having a training center in Beijing on calf care, milk quality control, vaccinations, foot care and other best practices for farms allows us to build connections."

Surveys were sent to some of the distributors that work with World Wide Sires in 2013 asking for comments in advance of Select Sires 50th anniversary. Some of those comments are listed here to give a taste of the appreciation that a farmer-owned cooperative in Plain City, Ohio has around the world.

Eddy Tierens from Belgium began selling Select Sires semen in 1980. He lists BLACKSTAR as the sire with the most impact in Holstein history and was the No. 1 TPI sire in 1989 when Eddy began his career as a classifier at VRV. He credits BLACKSTAR with changing the typical Friesian cow on Flemish farms to real, dairy Holstein cows. Eddy also mentions that he is proud that he can sell the top sires of the breed and that even though Select's stud code is 7; they are always No. 1 to him.

Adolf Langhout of the Netherlands began handling Select Sires semen 28 years ago and credits the people at Select Sires for building one of the best A.I. studs in the world and the bulls for keeping Select Sires one of the leading studs worldwide.

Markus Hitz began selling Select Sires semen in Switzerland in 1972. He has used bulls from BLACKSTAR to GLEN and considers Select Sires the most successful A.I. organization worldwide because of the different product lineups like proven bulls, genomic bulls and sexed semen offerings.

In Italy, Renato Santuari, Ph.D., has been selling for Select Sires since 1974 covering such bulls as GLENDELL and ELEVATION to O MAN and PLANET. He credits Select Sires with bringing real genetic improvement to Italy much to the great satisfaction of customers.

Maurice Naber passes along thoughts from Jordan, where he has handled Select Sires semen since 2004. He lists 7HO7650 JACKSON and 7HO8036 MASTER as two bulls of influence because they greatly improved fertility in Jordan and helped him build his market. He mentions the "green straw" as unique and most acceptable, and says the credibility, reliability and ranking of Select Sires sets it apart.

In the Czech Republic, Mirek Novotny has handled Select Sires semen for 23 years and lists BLACKSTAR as the most impressive sire, O MAN as the most influential sire, PLANET as the best outcross sire and MILLION as the highest fertility sire. He mentions that he is very proud to have worked with the most stable and most influential A.I. company in the world for the last 23 years. Novotny mentions the famous history, excellent utilization of genomics and latest biotechnology of reproduction that makes Select Sires the highest level you can work for.

Zoltan Supek has marketed Select Sires semen in Hungary since 1995 and his company Holstein Genetika, Ltd. began a joint venture with World Wide Sires in 1990, thanks to political and economic changes. Supek mentions that the formal relationship began in 1990 but the national animal breeding organization administered by the communist government actually had worked with Select Sires semen through WWS much earlier. The sires that he mentioned would be recognizable to any cutting-edge dairy breeder today in the U.S. He praises Select Sires for bringing the first sexed semen to Hungary in 2006 and for having sires on both sides of the pedigree of the 2012 national show

Joel Mergler in Middle East training dairy producers.

winner in an O MAN x BLITZ daughter. "The Select Sires bull program, just like their management and technical staff, have always produced a firm background for us," said Supek.

The Livestock Entrepreneurs Association of Albania has been using Select Sires semen since 2002 and commends Select Sires for the training and technology that are helping the "small and poor conditioned farms of Albania" to start using elite bulls and sexed semen technology. In China, the WWS division echoes comments like this that Select Sires genetics and technical expertise in "pursuing genetic perfection."

Hubertus Diers has marketed Select Sires semen for WWS Germany since 1994 and lists the integrity, reliability, friendship and great sires of Select Sires as a big reason for improvement. In Russia, Natalia Sinitcyna has handled Select Sires semen since 1999 for the Association ASCHAR. To her, Select Sires has been an innovator for "new technologies for work improvement, new programs for successful work on farms, good bulls, good value for a quality product and a wide variety of sexed semen."

In 1984, NOSAWA & Co, Ltd. began handling Select Sires semen in Japan and Sho Yoshida shares these comments. "We have imported bovine semen from overseas for 30 years and Select Sires' bulls have dominated other bulls during this period and improved Japanese dairy cattle," said Yoshida. These comments are echoed by Wade Pringle who has marketed Select Sires semen in South Africa since 1991 "Select bulls have proven to be consistent to their data over the years and have fit well into the various systems we have marketed in," said Pringle. "Their bulls have given us the marketing edge over competitors."

Tommie Eriksson of Skanesemin, Sweden shares that he has marketed Select Sires semen since 1984 and the high production and the good type of the sires is always there. Finally, perhaps Gilles Florid of BOVEC in France says it best. "Select Sires is an organization that is controlled by dairy farmers and it is great to see that all of its employees keep that in mind all the time, and are doing their best to serve the farmer base," said Florid. "I particularly appreciate the extraordinary passion, knowledge and dedication of the Select Sires people I work with, but even more, one has to appreciate that they are humble and easy to talk to."

Select Sires exists for the benefit of its customers. Whether that customer is in Wisconsin or Albania, it shows that a common bond among dairy and beef cattle breeders exists. Famed cattle sale pedigree man Horace Backus has a saying "buy the best and breed them better!" From Japan to South Africa and from Sweden to Jordan, breeders across the world are breeding them better with Select Sires.

Annual Report 1991

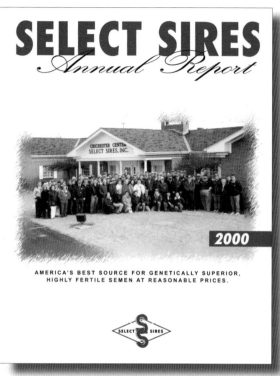

SELECT SIRES
Annual Report

2000

AMERICA'S BEST SOURCE FOR GENETICALLY SUPERIOR, HIGHLY FERTILE SEMEN AT REASONABLE PRICES.

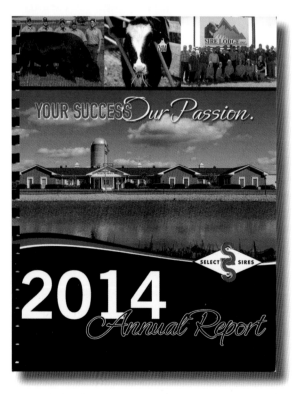

YOUR SUCCESS *Our Passion.*

2014 *Annual Report*

As Select Sires began the next quarter-century of the cooperative in 1990, 4,780,140 units were sold. The first year of the new millennium and Dave Thorbahn as CEO in 2000 saw 6,835,992 units marketed and growth continued to 14,763,533 units sold in 2014.

13

• • •

Planning the Roadmap for the Future

◆ ◆ ◆

The popular business management book, "Good to Great" by Jim Collins, talks first about getting the right people on the bus, getting the people in the right seats and then giving those participants the right products to deliver. For Select Sires, the first 25 to 35 years had a real focus on getting the right people on the bus, meaning the right mix of member cooperatives that could cover the marketing of Select Sires across the nation with the leaders in place to get it done. The last 15 to 25 years of Select Sires have focused on having the correct product for the customer and developing or acquiring the new product if it did not exist. The strong base of local-led leadership at the individual member cooperatives is a real asset and it has only been enhanced with the innovations that have been introduced through the last 15 years and the new innovations being worked on at Select Sires.

As Select Sires prepares for the next 50 years, the focus will remain to work cooperatively with the member-owners to feed a hungry world and the challenge will only be greater. In 1965, the global population was 3.3 billion people, in 2015 the global population is 7.2 billion people, and the projection is for the world to reach nine billion people by 2040. To feed these additional mouths, agriculture will have to become more productive. Agriculture will have to improve yields as the potential growth in arable land

Innovative Solution to Inbreeding.

stands at 5 percent with a 12 percent increase happening in developing countries, but an 8 percent reduction in arable land for developed countries. This means that the role Select Sires has played in maximizing every part of the dairy and beef enterprise only becomes more important as efficiencies need to be gained and yields need to be maximized. Select Sires is a forward-looking company, the board of directors have always challenged management and the leaders of the cooperative to innovate new solutions, and history shows that Select Sires will be up to the task.

The board and leadership operate under two guiding principles when looking at the future course of Select Sires, first that there is a strong future for agriculture and secondly that we have the ability to feed the world. The rules will be different than in the past, as the arable land is limited and new measurements such as carbon footprint and nutrient impact will be monitored. But the ability to innovate solutions will not waver as evidenced by Chief Executive Officer David Thorbahn's report to the membership in the Fall 2014 edition of the Selections magazine. "Crop farming is now using precision techniques like satellite imaging that can plan fertilizer, seed and pesticide applications by the acre and yard," said Thorbahn. "Dairy and beef industries are moving to these types of approaches by providing data to manage every cow individually." He then explains that the CowManager monitoring system offered by Select Sires can offer real-time data on the cow for activity, rumination, temperature, feeding time and location all in an ear tag. It is an investment in labor management for the farms of the member-owners of Select Sires. The most effective labor is educated labor. By offering useful data to the manager and employees of the farm, decisions can be made that improve yields, keep cattle productive and increase profitability.

The board of directors also made an investment in future opportunities for Select Sires when they approved a new position, chief development officer, in 2012. The person that filled that position is Todd Kranz and his duties focus on leading the execution of strategic planning initiatives and overseeing customer service strategies. This was a bold move to have a position focused on the opportunities that exist for Select Sires to offer new products and solutions to the membership. New opportunities that arose just in 2014 include the River Valley Farm partnership, the acquisition of GenerVations Inc. and formation of Select Sires GenerVations in Canada and a partnership with Wulf Cattle on the Breeding to Feeding program. All initiatives expanded the reach of Select Sires to new markets and offered additional opportunities to existing markets.

Innovation takes research, and Select Sires has partnered with leading universities to develop a new generation of leaders that can continue to develop solutions and opportunities for the customer. Dr. Matt Utt, director of research at Select Sires, is one of these leaders. Dr. Utt joined Select Sires in 2014 after a stint as a research associate at Select Sires in 2012. Through a partnership with The Ohio State University and the Select Sires C.E. Marshall Graduate Research Associateship, Dr. Utt was able to complete his doctorate in reproductive physiology and animal sciences while working with Select Sires. The pool of leaders studying semen collection, freezing, extenders, evaluation procedures and semen fertility potential is limited, but this partnership helps to get talented, young people on a path where they can work for Select Sires in developing new solutions for the membership.

Select Sires focus on the future of dairy management includes a commitment to monitoring systems that allow for precision herd management.

Some of these new solutions will also be of the genetic variety, as much opportunity exists in regions of the world just developing their dairy and beef markets. The growth in arable land that can occur is generally in Latin America and sub-Saharan

Africa. Those climates take a special kind of animal and Select Sires is already at work developing a breed of cow that will maximize the ability to produce meat and milk in those tropical areas. This genetic research also builds on research for sexed semen and strategies for maximizing genetic progress from your best cattle. Whether the cow resides in Ecuador or Kansas, every breeder wants to populate his or her herd from the best genetics available for the environment. Inventory management strategies being developed by Select Sires with research from Penn State University are helping breeders systematically decide the best strategies for how to breed their cattle. Select Sires is there to work with the customer every step of the way including identifying the correct mix of embryos, sexed semen and beef genetics.

One thing is for certain, the dairy and beef markets will look quite different when Select Sires celebrates its 75th anniversary in 2040. A cooperative like Select Sires does not spend much time looking at the past, except when you can learn from it. The history of Select Sires tells us that a continual effort will be made to have the best people in the industry and find innovative solutions that benefit the membership. That innovation may come along in the form of genetics, reproductive technology, service strategies or a host of other opportunities that Select Sires is developing. Some of the opportunities have not even been discovered because the issue has not been presented yet by the growing world. Select Sires exists for one reason, and one reason only, to benefit the member-owner. Working together, Select Sires will help the member-owner feed the world.

About the Author

Kirk Sattazahn grew up on a family dairy farm in Berks County, Pennsylvania and developed an appreciation for Select Sires at an early age. A 7HO543 Carlin-M Ivanhoe BELL daughter he acquired from his uncle as a calf went on to become his first Excellent cow and the first Excellent cow on the farm. Later, a daughter of 7HO2235 OCOLTER Chairman Monitor, which he bred, became his farm's first homebred Excellent.

After graduating from Penn State University with an Agricultural Business Management degree in 1994, Kirk was hired by Sire Power and joined the Select Sires family in 2000 where he is currently director of marketing for Select Sire Power.

A graduate of the Young Dairy Leaders Institute and a frequent contributor to Hoard's Dairyman magazine, Kirk now owns the family dairy farm with his wife Stephanie and their five children.

7H195 Wapa Arlinda CONDUCTOR

7H191 WAYNE-Spring Fond Apollo

7H477 GLENDELL Arlinda Chief

7H58 Round Oak Rag Apple ELEVATION

USDA (5/77)   99%R + 1,411M + 46F +$130
HFAA (2/77)   99%R + 1.73PDT

7HO980 Walkway Chief Mark (VG-87)

7HO2236 Emprise Bell Elton (EX-95)

7HO543 Carlin-M Ivanhoe Bell (EX-93)

7HO1897 To-Mar Blackstar-ET (EX-93)

...head of his
...tein

Impact sire
of the 1990s

SETTING THE
STANDARD FOR
EXCELLENCE

You can hang your hat on it!

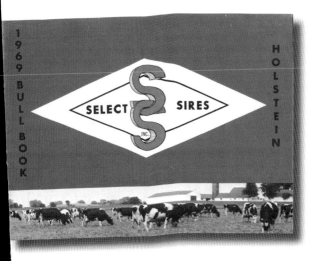

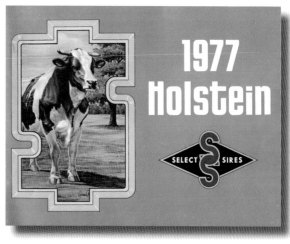

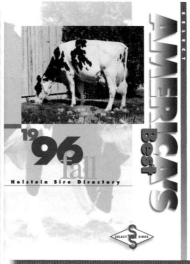

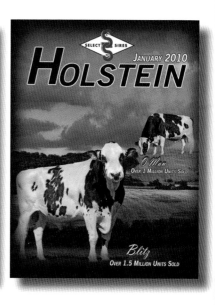

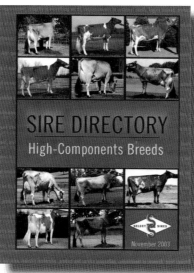

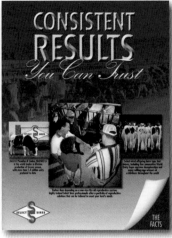

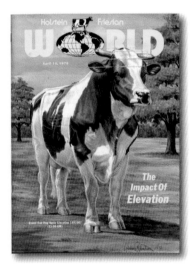

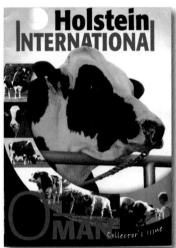

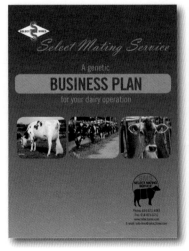